Handbook
for the
Emerging
Woman

Handbook
for the
Emerging
Woman

A manual for awakening
the unlimited power
of the
feminine spirit

Mary Elizabeth Marlow

THE
DONNING COMPANY
PUBLISHERS
NORFOLK/VIRGINIA BEACH

The Donning Company/Publishers
5659 Virginia Beach Boulevard
Norfolk, Virginia 23502

Edited by DeAnna L. Gladieux
Book design by Patrick Smith
Adapted illustrations by Sherri Faye Dugan

Library of Congress Cataloging-in-Publication Data   a:

Marlow, Mary Elizabeth, 1940-
    Handbook for the emerging woman.

    1. Women—Psychology. I. Title.
HQ1206.M344   1988   305.4'2   88-18076
ISBN 0-89865-672-9 (pbk.)

Printed in the United States of America

To the women who have
opened their hearts
and shared deeply
of their grief and wounds,
their joys and triumphs.
All of them
have taught me well
about the profound,
endless transformative power
of women.

Contents

The Bitch is that part of us that is connected to our feelings of powerlessness. We nag, grouch, whine, withdraw, shout, or shut down because we don't feel we have other options. Once we learn how to clearly identify and name our Bitch, we are able to move decisively to our real power and true identity.

The Dragon Fight is the struggle we have with ourselves when we reject and rebel against our parents or strive to emulate them. Learning to identify both the obvious and the hidden "Dragons" allows us to understand our female-male polarity and our relationship patterns.

Betrayal is the death of trust. It is important to know how we set ourselves up for betrayal experiences, what we can learn from them (don't waste a good betrayal!), and how we can move beyond pain and grief to empower ourselves.

The ability to transform life's experiences is not new. It has been known in many ancient cultures, including the Native American. They have a respect and understanding of the power of the four elements. As women, we too can tap into the transformational energy of these elements.

The pantheon of Greek goddesses reflects the diversity and complexity within women and provides us with a new way of looking at ourselves from a perspective which is thoroughly feminine. Until very recently, these archetypes have been lost to Western culture. As we awaken and search for wholeness, the goddesses return to help us in our journey.

Preface

I am sitting on a rock overlooking the Aegean Sea which shimmers with crystal highlights under the clear, cobalt, sunlit sky of Greece. In the background, a donkey is braying and the warm, gentle breeze carries the welcome sound of laughter and giggles of the village children at play. How appropriate it is for me to be here at this time, in this ancient land whose goddesses even now speak so profoundly to women.

Today is my birthday. Birthdays are a time for celebration and reflection. And as I celebrate my birth, I lead a week-long seminar, assisting women from many countries in their new birth with insights and processes that have taken me years to realize.

I feel blessed.

And I reflect. How did it happen? The progression of events seems so natural that I have seldom paused to marvel at its specialness. In many ways, my journey has been predictable and sequential, and yet, I am aware of all the events, people, and circumstances that have paraded through my life in such a short time, initiating so many significant inner changes. Just ten years ago, barely a decade, I was a housewife living a limited, stereotyped existence in a spacious home on Virginia's James River. Now I am doing what I love most, leading seminars, lecturing, counseling women (and men) in many parts of the world, traveling, learning, growing, supporting myself, feeling fulfilled with many loving relationships.

As I sit, I feel a smile rising from deep within. There is a profound joy in just being.

Acknowledgements

It was clear, almost from the beginning, that this was not just my book, but would indeed be an "aquarian conspiracy." The right people, situations, stories, and talents appeared at precisely the right moment to play out a divine synchronicity from start to finish, as though to acknowledge that the hand of the Divine Mother was indeed guiding the direction of the book. It seemed necessary, as well, that a unique and diverse assortment of people play particular roles in its creation, giving credence to an unseen alchemy at work which required a combination of various kinds of energies so that, in the end, this would be a handbook that could serve a broad spectrum of women. Both the stories and the people are real; only the names have been changed to protect privacy.

It has not just been women who have played a role in this book, symbolic of the importance of female-male polarity and acknowledgement that men also can be sensitive to the special issues that belong just to women. A heartfelt thanks, first, to Robert Krajenke, who helped smooth out many a wrinkle in the manuscript with his assistance in writing and editing, and particularly for his patience enduring my erratic changes. A special acknowledgement to Bud Ramey, who has expanded my understanding of friendship and who consistently helped hold the vision of the book. Without him this would probably still be an unwritten manuscript.

In Europe there was the special blessing of Elinore Detiger, otherwise and rightfully known as the "Global Mother" who, using her innate cosmic time clock, would appear in fairy-godmother fashion at just the right moment with just the right magic potion. From Holland, it was Manec van der Lugt and the nurturing energy of the women of the Davidhuis who gave constant and consistent support. It was within the beautiful walls of my home away from home that I was lovingly coaxed and encouraged so that much of the birthing process of this book could take place.

I wish to acknowledge Peter for his assistance in the initial stages of the book and particularly for the knowledge that he has so generously imparted over the years, giving me a thorough grounding in spiritual principles. Jason, thank you for opening my heart and for being my initiator into mysticism. Francis Allen, you have been my brother on the path. I appreciate your honesty and wisdom and value your role as both friend and catalyst as you have encouraged me to face the other side of myself. I particularly want to acknowledge your insights and generous assistance with this book. And finally, thank you to Dr. Carl Simonton and Stephanie Simonton, from whom I learned much about the transformational process possible within each of us.

There were a whole host of others who, in unique ways, added their own specialness: Carol Bush, co-creator of the original version of the Emerging Woman seminar; Grace Davide, who helped edit from the feminine perspective and always added a graceful touch; Cheri Sommers, number one assistant and cheerleader; Marleen Kaptein, infinitely resourceful Girl Friday; Nicole Dupont, an important booster in the beginning stages; Jean Reeder and Martha Hamilton, reliable sounding boards; DeAnna Gladieux, a young woman with insight beyond her years; and Paul Schnavel, to whom we are indebted for the cover photograph.

There were countless others who contributed with their life stories, ever expanding my vision of what it is to be a woman, and still others who gave their encourage-ment and well wishes with, "When is the book coming out?" or, "I know it is going to be good."

Finally, I value my roots, especially my parents, Guy and Esther Marlow, who were not perfect parents and who were the perfect parents for me. And to my two sons David and John, I have been sustained by your love and encouragement. I especially appreciate your comment, after reading the manuscript; "Now we know why it took you so long. We're really proud of you." That made it all worthwhile.

Introduction

To experience all that a woman can be is an incredible joy. Sometimes, simply to touch, even if by accident, our previously unrealized and unrecognized depth and beauty gives us a tantalizing hint of what we truly are and of what we can become. We do experience these depths, but sometimes it is only through dreams and daydreams, without the realization that it is possible to live the dream. This handbook is about awakening those dreams, awakening the full depth, potency, and inner power of being a woman.

It is about women. It is about women's experiences—their weaknesses, their strengths, their challenges, their victories, their journeys toward knowing and loving themselves. You will meet many special women here, each one expressing her own use of the concepts and the theories within the context of daily living. New insight is useless without the understanding of how to apply it. The women mentioned here are real, and their stories are real-life examples.

This handbook should be used as a guide for women emerging into all they can be. It is not the only way but it is one which many women have found valuable and effective. It is based on the belief that we can choose to be a whole person, who is a woman, and that we can participate in the process of creating that reality.

The handbook is more than a collection of thoughts. It is an experience. Each chapter relates to an essential step, an initiation, through which every woman moves in her emerging process. These steps are graduated and build one upon another, with each chapter presenting at least one or more experiential processes for you to measure and validate your own progress. Your chronology may be slightly different than the one

suggested in the handbook, but you will resonate
with the steps.

The handbook is designed so it can be used
individually, or with two or more sisters, friends, or in a
support group. Your journey through the handbook can
be a private one, or a shared experience. The choice
is yours.

It is time to take ownership of our spiritual nature
and to claim our inner authority.

May your transformation be a joyful one!

The Bitch is the role or response we resort to when we don't know what else to do, when we don't know how to express what we are really feeling in a confident, whole way, or when we won't give ourselves permission to comment or say what we notice or observe as it occurs.

The Bitch is that part of us that is connected to our feelings of powerlessness. We nag, grouch, whine, withdraw, shout, or shut down because we don't feel we have other options.

We use the Bitch to manipulate and maneuver—and she usually gets results. But there are better ways to get the love and attention we deserve.

In this chapter, you will learn to clearly identify and name your Bitch, enabling you to move decisively to your real power and true identity.

CHAPTER 1

Owning
the Bitch

All women are magicians. Our magic is the innate
ability we have to both create and transform our
experience of life. As women, our only real choice is
whether we practice our magic consciously and how
much magic we are willing to use.

It has taken me many years to understand this
magic—the magic of a woman emerging from limitation
into wholeness and enjoying the freedom inherent in the
process. The insights came from my own journey as a
woman, as well as the experiences of many women I
have taught and counseled. It reflects the wisdom of
diverse women, from India to Greece, from Jerusalem to
Glastonbury, rich and poor, educated and unlettered.
Many female "teachers" have shared their insights with
me. They have been cancer patients struggling with
death as well as women groping their way out of confusion while seeking new identities and ways of living.
My teachers have been gifted and joyful women, angry
women, enraged women, women with visions and
dreams, those who are succeeding, those overwhelmed
by loss and change, and those who are numb with boredom and apathy. They have taught me about courage,
courage to move through darkness and rise—to claim
their true identity—renewed, empowered, and joyful.

Begin The Dance

The emerging process is a wonderful dance. It is a movement to wholeness and joy. There is a theme that continues to play throughout the dance and when you can hear that melody, it makes the movement easier, more graceful. The first step is to be willing to name the name: identify clearly where you are and what your issues are. Secondly, accept that where you are and what you have done up to this point is okay. Thirdly, be open to all the possibilities, potential, and power that is yours. The dance has many moods because you are intricate, complex, and delicate. And it will take you home to your heart where you can finally claim full ownership of your inner authority. Move at your own pace, at your own rhythm. You may want to leave some steps until later. They are ready for you when you are ready for them.

We begin with what may seem to be one of the most challenging steps, both in the book and in our life: Owning the Bitch. This chapter is placed at the beginning for that reason. If from the beginning we can establish honesty as a requirement, then the rest will come.

For now, drop preconceived ideas about the word Bitch. And be open to another view. We all know that we have parts inside that we wish weren't there, or that we are afraid are there, or that come out when we least want them to. It is these parts that I am boldly calling the Bitch. I choose this term because it is unattractive. If it is unattractive enough, we will have to notice it. We won't be able to avoid or deny or glamorize or whitewash her behavior. And secondly, the Bitch is not our real self but a caricature of our shadow self. Be mature enough to see the humor in what you do. We can really look ridiculous when we get into these patterns. What we won't resort to! Humor is healthy. We can be both responsible and lighthearted at the same time.

The Birth Of A Bitch

The winter had been especially cold with heavy snow. My brother John and my sister Joanna and I were constantly sneezing, dripping, and coughing and passing our colds back and forth to one another. So it was great news when Mom and Dad announced that the family was going for a vacation, to enjoy some warm Florida sun. At last, some real excitement.

On the way south, John and I were in the back seat, acting out that ancient sibling rivalry of claiming territorial rights. In fairness to John, I believe I started the fight with a few innocent jabs. John retaliated with some serious pokes. Our wrestling and pushing continued over the next few miles until we reached the restaurant, and then it spilled over into the menu-ordering ritual.

John squeezed my hand under the table, and bent my fingers back. My eyes began to water, and I squirmed in my seat. I was double-jointed and a lot of John's hand crunching I could tolerate without a squeal or whimper. But then he pulled too hard, and the pain became more than I could tolerate. I screamed and pulled my hand away.

Mother lowered her menu and gave us one of her stone cold glares.

"Betty, leave John alone," she said, fixing her eyes on me.

I was outraged! Who was being hurt—John or me? I was! Without a word, I pushed my chair back and stormed away from the table. I knew that if I exploded, I would be punished. I wanted to cry, but I couldn't. I wanted to scream, but I dared not.

"Oh, Betty's on her high horse again," I heard Mom say behind me as I walked away, and Dad smiled knowingly. Typical of many parents, they judged my behavior, but didn't know how to help me deal with it.

So many feelings were churning inside me. Frustration. Anger. Hurt. And no place to put them! Something inside me was pleading to be understood, to be reassured that I was still loved. I walked to the other end of the restaurant, trying to quiet these turbulent emotions, and when I had stuffed them down sufficiently to where I felt under control, I returned to the table and assumed my usual, passive, girlish attitude. The family approved, and I felt accepted. But inside, there was a live volcano ready to erupt.

A man at the next table stood up to pay his bill, and as he passed our table, he stopped to pay his compliments. "You have such an attractive family," he remarked to my mother and father. And then, winking at me, he added, "That little one is something else. She's quite an actress."

A bitch was born. I was three years old at the time.

***

The Bitch is our false self, and a false self can only give false power. The Bitch is something we create to cover up our fears because we lack confidence in our true selves. Settling for the Bitch is a poor alternative to making decisions for ourselves and expressing our own real feelings and needs.

***

The Bitch Grows Up

At age three, it never occurred to me that I was cheating myself by creating a Bitch. In fact, it took many years to realize that the false part, the role or disguise I had assumed as a three year old sitting at that table with a smile while my insides were burning, was separate from the self that is the Real Me.

Thirty-five years later I looked at my Bitch square in the face, and realized what I had created.

It was a hot June day, and I was upstairs in the bedroom of our spacious home on the James River, sorting out socks. The weather was humid and sticky. The cooling system had broken so the windows were open to capture whatever little breeze might stir in hopes it would relieve some of the oppressive heat.

Sock-sorting is a mindless task, and my thoughts were dancing among some pleasant dreams when suddenly my husband Sean bounded through the door, bringing a feeling of urgent energy into the room. Often this energy, which was so typical of him, was a delightful change; other times it felt like an intrusion. Today was one of those days.

Sean started commenting on the condition of the garden, and usually this would spark my interest. But today, as he droned on about the zinnias and the broccoli, I just kept sorting and folding, sorting and folding, pretending to be involved and interested in his monologue.

And then I heard Sean say, "Well, what do you think?"

What did I think? About what! I had no idea what he had been talking about!

I started to stammer some vague response, and then, my stomach knotted. It was as if a complete stranger had just walked into my bedroom—a man off the street—and said, "You've been married to me for fifteen years."

My hands turned cold and wet, sticking to the socks I kept carefully sorting. "And I am a stranger to him." A sick shiver went through my body.

Over the years, I had tried so hard to please him.

To adjust. To adapt. To fit in. We never fought, we never argued. But what had become of the imaginative, adventurous me who was full of fire and spontaneous emotion, or the young child who had felt such curiosity and wonder? We had what everyone considered an enviable situation. Sean was the successful attorney/husband. We had two fine sons, lived in the most exclusive part of town, and were members in good standing in the Episcopal Church, the Junior League, and the country club. But why did I feel empty and unfulfilled?

For the first time, I realized the knotted stomach and clammy hands, the tense body, shallow smile, and tilted chin was the Bitch I had created. She was a whole set of reactions that came when I didn't know what to do or what to say. I had been living with this unknown Bitch ever since I sat down at the table on our way to Florida—and I was still stuck there, swallowing my feelings and doing everything that was pleasing and pleasant to get what I thought I wanted. No wonder Sean was a stranger. I was a stranger to myself!

I recognized the Bitch inside me and, at the same time, I knew it wasn't who I really was. But I needed to name her. I needed to get a handle on what she was like. The label had to suit the particular quality, the pattern or syndrome, that she represented for me. A name came instantly to mind. The Pleasing Passive. That's what I had become. In due time the socks got sorted, but I had a more serious sorting out to do.

The Bitch Must Be Faced

The Bitch is the negative ego, the cover-up we create when we are afraid. Afraid that if people really knew who we are or what we have done, what we are thinking or feeling, they wouldn't love us, they wouldn't accept or approve of us. The only trouble is, if we call upon her enough times, eventually she becomes an automatic response.

As children we learned that if being cute and smiling doesn't work, sulking, pouting, and silence may eventually get Mom and Dad to give us attention. Or, we might break through by kicking and screaming, ranting and raving, until we wear our parents down and they give us the attention we want out of frustration. Or we might simply decide to be "nice"—at all costs.

What Happens If We Don't Acknowledge The Bitch?

It is hard to admit that we possess a Bitch, or Bitches. In fact, we will usually deny, repress, rationalize, or suppress our behavior just to prove she doesn't exist.

Failure to acknowledge our Bitch means we will continue to feel powerless, suppressed, unfulfilled—and afraid. The Bitch is the defense against our insecurities, and we call on her to help us manipulate and maneuver to get *what we think we want* from others. If we need attention, recognition, and reassurance in order to cover over our fears, she gets it for us. At that level she is very effective. Except what she gets for us doesn't last. And we need to get it again and again, which keeps us stuck in the same negative patterns.

The Bitch Must Be Confronted

Unwillingness to confront the Bitch usually means we find a way to recognize her in others. A parent, a partner, a boss, or a friend presents us with all the negative patterns that we deny within ourselves. They act out our disowned parts. In other words, if we don't deal with the inner Bitch, we'll draw one to us. What we dislike in others is within ourselves.

When a family group fails to acknowledge the shadow self, one family member invariably will act out the "craziness" by doing everything the others deny or pretend they don't have. This is the proverbial "black sheep" of the family.

On a slightly larger scale, when a community fails to come to grips with its negative unconscious patterns, it projects them on to a scapegoat—the Salem Witch trials is a classic case in point. In modern times, it is the Jews, Blacks, and immigrants who sometimes become the target for projections and the twentieth century scapegoats.

How To Meet The Bitch

One of the classic challenges in the ancient myths and fairy tales is meeting the hideous damsel, the step-mother, an evil fairy, or a witch. She is the one with the power to turn the hero/heroine into stone, or put them to sleep, or cause them to lose their heads. Nothing significant happens in these tales without that kind of confrontation. The Witch, or Bitch is the catalyst for change.

There are some subtleties in meeting the Witch. Though she often appears as an obvious hag, dark and sinister with a bent, disfigured body, crackling voice, and beady eyes, other times she disguises herself in forms that appear harmless, alluring, or seductive. Snow White, for example, was tricked into eating the poisonous apple because her evil mother-in-law disguised herself as a harmless old woman.

In many fairy tales, the Witch is encountered in the depths of a dark green forest, a murky and sinister place. It takes courage to enter it, and often the pathway back or out is lost. Hansel and Gretel carefully leave a trail of bread crumbs behind them, and birds eat them up. It is as though, once the decision has been made to meet her, there is no turning back!

As women, we too must be willing to go into our own dark green Forest of the Unconscious to meet the shadow shelf, the negative feminine. The confrontation and acknowledgement of that part of the psyche is an important step in the process of becoming whole.

Every woman, on her path to wholeness, has the same challenges of initiation, integration, and transformation as the characters in the old folktales. The murky, ominous forest where the Bitch is met is the darkness of our own unconscious, which we fear to enter. But until we do, the Witch's power is unchallenged.

The Power Of The Name

One way to defuse the power of the Bitch is to identify her, to name her.

The belief in the power of names runs through almost all religions, and in many myths, fairy tales, and legends. Knowing words of power attend great events and, as with Ali Baba, open doors magically.

One of the best illustrations of this ancient principle is from Grimm's fairytale, Rumpelstiltskin.

A poor miller foolishly boasts to the king that his daughter can spin straw into gold. The king, ever eager for more wealth, immediately puts her to the test. He locks her in a room filled with straw and a spinning wheel, and demands that she turn the straw into gold.

The terrified girl sits at her spinning wheel, sobbing and wailing with no idea how to proceed when a curious little dwarf appears and offers his magic. However, she must agree to make payment for his help.

*The first time the dwarf asks for her necklace,
which she gladly gives—and he spins the straw into gold.*

*The next morning, when the greedy king discovers
the room is filled with gold, he orders more straw
brought in, and demands she turn it to gold.*

*The dwarf appears again, and asks for her ring. She
agrees, and again the dwarf turns the straw to purest
gold. When the king returns, he is ecstatic and has the
room filled with more straw than before, and orders her
to spin again.*

*When the dwarf appears, this time he demands
her first-born child as his due. She agrees because she
has nothing left to give.*

*In the morning, the king is so pleased with all the
gold, he marries the miller's daughter. Within a year
they have a child.*

*One day, as she is rocking her newborn son, the
dwarf comes to collect his payment. She pleads with
him to keep her child. And moved to pity by her tears,
he offers a way out. If she can discover his name within
three days, she can keep her child.*

*For three days, she plays a desperate guessing
game with the dwarf, trying to discover his name, but
without success. On the third day, the queen's faithful
servant discovers the dwarf's home high in the mountains at the end of the forest and spies unnoticed while
the dwarf dances gleefully around the fire, chanting
"Rumpelstiltskin is my name."*

*In the evening, the dwarf comes to the palace to
claim the child. He asks the queen for the last time to tell
him his name. When she pronounces the word of
power, "Rumpelstiltskin," the dwarf destroys himself in
a rage.*

In fairytales as in dreams, a dwarf can represent

"stunted growth," an aspect of unfulfilled potential which exists within the unconscious. As long as his name was a secret—his true essence or identity concealed—Rumpelstiltskin called the shots.

Once the miller's daughter "named the name," she got to keep her child—the symbol of her personal power. The principle illustrated here is that when we can name or identify something, we gain power over it. To know the name of a person, object, or situation is to correctly identify its essence. And by knowing its essence you can establish an effective relationship with it. When I recognized my Bitch as a "Pleasing Passive," I identified a false part of myself that I was using to gain acceptance, love, and appreciation. Knowing her name, I could dismiss her power and diminish her influence. It was a step toward creating real power.

Name Your Bitch

In this section, you will have an opportunity to claim power—the power of "naming" the Bitch.

Most people, from time to time, have expressed the behavior of one or more of the Bitches described below, and no doubt one or two will strike a particularly familiar note in you. As you read, recognize which ones most describe your behavior, and then try "Naming The Bitch" at the end of the chapter.

Bitches come in many guises. There are Bitches to suit every temperament, personality, and preference. Bitches abound!

The Bitches

ICY MAIDEN

"I said there's nothing wrong." (But you better

know how I feel anyway).

She is the woman who is cold, unattainable, sometimes haughty. She keeps her power by withholding her energy. Her heart is hidden and closed off. Her fear—although it may be subconscious—is that if she ever really opens herself up she will be used or abandoned. The Icy Maiden creates a sense of safety for herself by shutting off her feelings. This Bitch avoids strong emotions. Anger, resentments, embarrassment, helplessness, etc., only produce conflicts and discomfort.

So, she decides not to feel anything at all. By avoiding her feelings, she gets to keep her control. Icy stares, folded arms, the "pull-away," and pursed lips are all a part of her game.

"Nothing is wrong," is her cold shut down. The game she plays is called, "You're supposed to love me enough to know what's wrong without my telling you—and if you don't, I'm going to shut down even more." The game is subtle, deliberate, and carefully executed.

It is as if to say, "I won't give myself to you because I'm not getting what I want from you."

CASTRATING FEMALE

"Wait 'til I get through with this son of a bitch!"

The Castrating Female is powerful and ruthless, sarcastic, disempowering, and belittling. She takes great delight in emasculating men with her sharp tongue, testy jabs, and barbs, or with a look, or through body language. Her sting is often felt in a message like this, "Oh, George, now really!" or, "You're going to do what? You've got to be kidding!"

She shows great disgust toward her mate. After all, "He's not a real man, just a wimp!" As long as she keeps him "lifeless," she can feel powerful.

THE SHRIEKING WAR GODDESS

"Just what the hell do you mean by that!"

The Shrieking War Goddess is highly manipulative and overpowering. Filled with explosive anger and enormous rage, she rants and raves to get control, and attacks at the slightest provocation.

No matter who is plundered and raped in the process, she challenges, "Let's get it all out!," often amidst yells and screams. As one woman in a workshop boasted, "I don't have a bit of trouble with anger. I just let it out." And she did—at a great cost to all around her.

Women who have suppressed their rage for years often harbor a Shrieking War Goddess. They have not learned to deal with issues as they come up. Instead they avoid trouble until their suppressed rage becomes powerful enough. Then the dam bursts, and the flood is enormous.

MERCILESS MERMAID

"Come and get me . . . . if you can."

These mythological creatures are half fish, half woman. The mermaid is the epitome of heartless, impersonal eroticism. Her aim is to conquer men, not for love, but for a craving to gain power. Her rage and desire to disempower is disguised by an exceedingly personable manner and apparent concern. The "Mermaid" is the proverbial "cock-tease" who only craves the game.

The power in wanting to be wanted is secondary to her greatest power, which lies in turning the man down at the critical moment, or just shutting her own energy off, and watching his confusion. Often, this pattern is a result of abusive exploitation early in life and it is an attempt to "get back" at men in general.

SACCHARINE BELLE

"Why honey, everything is just fine."

We associate this Bitch with the deep South, but, in truth, she is found everywhere. Everything is sweet and sugary to the point of being repugnant. Real feelings and opinions are covered by a sugar-coated exterior shell. But it is not real sugar, just a "substitute." It is all a role, a superficial game. The smile is plastic, the conversation predictable.

"Well, how are you? I am so glad to see you."

"And how is your mother? Really, I am so glad!"

"Now you really must come and see us. We would love to see you!"

The little magnolia blossom has charmed every-one, though there is little real caring in the script. It is often effective. It does work, and it gets results, including important invitations and the prestige of being "in" with the right people. Scarlett O'Hara in *Gone With The Wind* knew quite well how to become the Saccharine Belle when she needed something for her beloved plantation, Tara.

SUFFERING MARTYR

"That's all right. . . . (sigh) . . . . I'll do it."

She is the woman who prides herself on stoic self-denial, martyring herself for her husband, her children, "the Cause," or her career. She holds back her anger, her sexuality, and suppresses her joy. She wins her points by suffering the most and letting everybody be aware of how much she hurts.

She believes suffering makes her special and chooses the opportune moments to sigh loudly as she starts to clear the table after a big meal. She vacuums noisily, or straightens up the room when the rest of the family is watching the Superbowl just so everybody will see "good ol' mom" working away again.

One woman who recalls playing the role of the Suffering Martyr quite well related that she prepared the family's Thanksgiving dinner with enough seats for everyone except herself. When asked where she was going to sit, she replied; "Oh, no, I won't sit down. I just want to be sure that everyone else is taken care of."

Everyone feels obligated to a Suffering Martyr. She dominates through her pain. From this highly manipulative and controlling position, she wields a lot of power. Veiled behind the suffering is usually a belief that she doesn't deserve love and nurturing.

She has yet to learn that she doesn't need to suffer to get love.

This behavior presents a seeming paradox that must be understood. True giving is a virtue that must come from a generous heart. If we give to impress others or to appear virtuous, we are operating with an ulterior motive. If we give because we feel we're supposed to, it's hell. Then we are indeed the Suffering Martyr.

PLEASING PASSIVE

"Whatever you say, dear."

Quiet, demure, agreeable, and compliant, this Bitch copes by becoming invisible, by not being noticed, or by not making waves or demands. The Pleasing Passive has given up original thought and personal opinions in the hope that she will not be objectionable and lose the approval of others.

One of the most startling examples of the Pleasing Passive was in a workshop that I was conducting in Holland. We were doing an exercise in which one partner allows another to push them until they turn around, face their partner directly, and say, "Stop, that's enough!" Body language and the manner in which the words are delivered reveal much about how a woman deals with her anger. In this particular instance, one woman allowed herself to be pushed clear across the room, and then turned and politely said. "Thank you." Our ingrained patterns run deep!

Usually, enormous rage is locked up behind the Pleasing Passive pattern. A very sweet, but painfully sad young woman once came to me, hunched over and suffering from migraine headaches. When she was growing up, her father had abused her both physically and emotionally. She was angry and terrified of expressing any anger, since her only model for expressing deep-felt emotions had been such a negative one.

To defuse the volcano that wanted to erupt, she needed a safe environment within which to experience her deep pain. Once trust was established between the two of us, we put a pillow on a bed and she began to pummel that pillow with her fists. She continued beating the pillow until her hurt and grief were vented. Suddenly, her migraine completely cleared. Releasing her long repressed anger was an important first step for her. The rest of the session focused on learning constructive ways for her to deal with feelings and to communicate effectively.

THE SEDUCTIVE SIREN

"This one's a challenge, but I'll get him."

In the myth *Odysseus,* Circe warns Odysseus not to be lured by the song of the Sirens, the enticing sounds sung by the maidens on the islands which they would pass. Circe knew that these Sirens led to the undoing of men. Nevertheless, Odysseus's men are lured onto the island and seduced into a powerless state where sex and pleasure rule.

The Seductive Siren is out to seduce men into sexual encounters, so she uses all of her feminine charms to entice and interest them. She wants the attention of men for the assurance of her own sexuality and to gain importance in the eyes of other women. Though she does give freely of her body, she holds back her inner self. Her game is not real intimacy, but conquest. Yet she wonders, "Am I still attractive? Can I still get him?"

Remember, Cleopatra was so enticing that wars were waged on her behalf.

MOTHER SUPERIOR

"I told you so. If only you had listened."

She is self-righteous, a know-it-all who can back up all her opinions, and does not like to be questioned. The effect on others can be chilling. It is as though something inside you shrinks in her presence.

She maintains rigid control of herself and the situation. Her standards of right and wrong are very strict and she has very little tolerance for the "grey" areas. Mother Superiors are definitely the female drill sergeants and are stereotyped as mothers, school teachers, head nurses, camp counselors, and corporate executives. With her, there is an enormous need to be "right," and if she finds that she had made an error of judgement, she will go to great lengths to cover herself so that she won't appear wrong.

ARMORED AMAZON

"I'm as good as any man—and you better believe it!"

The Armored Amazon is that woman who identifies with the power aspect of the masculine. At the same time, she renounces the capacity to relate lovingly, a quality that has traditionally been associated with the feminine. Usually, these Amazon women are high achievers. They have made their way in the medical profession, the legal world, the world of stocks and bonds. They are as good or better than any man. Her masculine side is highly developed and provides for competence, confidence, and aggression, but the feminine side of softness and feeling is underdeveloped and repressed. According to Linda Leonard in *The Wounded Woman,* this Bitch is often the result of a wound in the father-daughter relationship, present in women whose fathers were "negligent or irresponsible, or not emotionally present."

Usually, there is a chink in the armor in this kind of woman, and if someone is allowed in that chink, she will have a great deal of difficulty dealing with emotional issues. The armor is her safeguard.

GOLD DIGGER

"He meets all of my qualifications—he's got lots of bucks."

Though more frequently found during an earlier period of history, Gold Diggers are still around. This woman is out for what she can get. If he doesn't have a Diner's Club card, membership in an elite country club, and a yacht, she is not interested. What can he buy for her? What will he give her? Real feelings of love are purely secondary. Money is where it's at. The Gold Digger, not knowing what real love is, settles for the greenbacks as her love substitute. Zsa Zsa Gabor has entertained us all with her stories of her millionaire husbands, proof that for some, "Diamonds are still a girl's best friend."

"I like it when they squirm."

This woman enjoys wounding the male. Her under-lying question is, "Do you love me enough to let me hurt you?" She methodically coaxes, then ensnares the man in her web. Once she has completed her ritual, she is ready for the lethal sting. It is deadly.

This pattern appears most frequently when a woman has been abused and rejected by her father. The wound is deep, and she wants revenge. Since her father is not around, she gets back at him through the males she encounters. She feels quite triumphant when she ends a relationship, leaving the man to deal with the pain and rejection.

In a counseling session recently, a young woman described in a rather cool manner, the great pain that her former partner was having because she decided to break off the relationship. There was almost a gleeful note in her description. He was suffering, and that proved he really loved her!

In her childhood, she shared a bedroom with her sister. Her father periodically came into the bedroom and had sexual relations with her sister. For years she felt rage at this abuse, but it wasn't until several sessions later that we uncovered the real cause of the rage. Her father hadn't chosen her!

With the termination of her relationship, she learned how much suffering she could cause. Though her father didn't love her enough to make her feel powerful, her suffering partner did. She had power to attract and destroy! This way, she could vicariously punish the father who hadn't chosen her.

"Maybe he's the one."

This is the classic little girl waiting for Prince Charming to come and rescue her. Or, as an older friend of mine put it, "Where the hell is Errol Flynn?" This Bitch believes that men have all the power and she has none. If she lucks into a worthwhile relationship, life can go well for her. If, on the other hand, she surrenders herself to a not-so-wonderful male, she will endure a lot of pain rather than be without a man.

Sarah, an attractive thirty-five-year-old woman is desperate because she has been divorced ten years and still—"no one!" Recently, she met an older man at a conference who was separated from his wife. There was immediate chemistry and they shared some magical time together. Now all of her hopes are built around the possibility that this time—this is it! She has considered relocating closer to him, even though his divorce is not yet final, and he has yet to start dealing with the many inner issues that come up after separation from a long-term relationship. If this new relationship doesn't turn out with a wedding and a tiered cake, she will be devastated. The Rescue Me Bitch constantly chooses to give her right to happiness over to men, and then, when it doesn't work out, feels unfairly victimized.

ALL FEATHERS AND NO BIRD

"Say, What?"

This female is daffy, disorganized, flighty, irrelevant, and undirected. Often she is imaginative, adventuresome, intuitive, and mystical. She can be quite engaging with her airy lightness. Goldie Hawn is often cast in this role in the movies. The underlying belief of many women who play this role is that it is not O.K. to be bright (so my intelligence must be camouflaged). This affected disguise is an attempt to be non-threatening to men, and the helplessness is quite disarming.

This bird warbles her flighty tunes to men, like this: "I never could read these instruction books. How do you work this thing?" or, "Does the key go here?. . I don't get it."

Many men want to be needed, and this damsel definitely appears to be in need of a man!

WILTING BITCH

"I give up. I can't handle it!"

The Wilting Bitch seems so helpless and loves to make you feel responsible for her.

"I can love everyone, but me. I am unworthy."

"Gee, you're wonderful, and I am just little ol' me."

She enjoys getting depressed. This way she gets others to come and rescue her by getting her out of her mood. If nobody rallies to her aid, she will remain inactive, depressed, and will bemoan the situation. Sometimes this bitch only shows herself in a crisis, remaining fully camouflaged at all other times.

RECONSTRUCTED BITCH

"I can really get into that."

She is the "New Age" groupie that has been through every process in the books. She has had her family reconstructed. She has been ESTed, Rolfed, Reikied, and Re-Birthed. She's had aromatherapy and Bach Remedies. She's been Gestalted, had psychic readings, and past life regressions. Her pastime is dropping names of the teachers and groups she knows and talking "the talk." The Reconstructed Bitch has it together, or so she wants to have everyone think. She comes to take the seminars and trainings, but not to learn from them. She knows it all, and has done it all—everything that is except change.

BITTER BITCH

"After all I did for you. . . . and what do I get?"

The Bitter Bitch hates herself. She is ugly to herself and to others. In some families, the Bitter Bitch is almost like an inheritance, something a bitter mother passes on to her daughters by filling their ears with her beliefs about how awful men and sex are. If her daughter should have any pain in her relationships with men, she will respond with the predictable "I told you so." She is right about being wronged and has an ax to grind.

A divorced woman, if she is the one who has been left, often plays the role of Bitter Bitch. A man's second wife can become a Bitter Bitch as well, especially if there are financial problems or troubles with the children of the first wife.

Deborah, an attractive thirty year old, closed her eyes and visualized her Bitch. She had named it, described it, and now the Bitch was right there with her. With a degree of courage, she visualized herself walking over to her bitch—a horrible, pathetic, wretched woman.

Deborah looked at this disgusting form and asked, "What is it that you want me to know? What do you need?"

The answer came back clearly to Deborah—"love and attention."

Part of her feminine spirit had been denied. Her inner woman felt martyred, sacrificed, and unwanted—and bitter as a result. All her woes came pouring out. With her imagination, holding the hands of this inner woman, Deborah poured all her love and caring into the pathetic form. The haggard old woman turned into a younger version of herself, vibrant, alive, energetic. The transformation was startling! When we can accept the negative self and love it, it no longer has power over us.

NAGGING BITCH

"For God's sake, Henry, put the top back on the toothpaste."

Nothing ever dies with the Nagging Bitch, and she never tires of trying to prove her point. She is the resurrector of the past—of old wounds, hurts, disappointments, and betrayals (real or imagined). The Nagging Bitch goes on and on about the same things. She carries a "Black Bag" full of past experiences. Critical, complaining, a whiner in relationships with men, she plays the hypercritical parent.

With unnerving accuracy, she knows just how to push your buttons.

TWO-FACED BITCH

"Of course, I will" . . . (You bastard, I'll get you for this!)

Two-Faced Bitches can be seen particularly in the corporate world. They are all smiles in your presence and all negativity behind your back. The Two-Faced Bitch really wants to ruin you, but you'd never suspect it. She wouldn't reveal her true feelings for the world. The face she puts on may be very pretty, and her words are almost always what you want to hear; but there is a seething conflict underneath. She is the daughter-in-law who plays well when the parents are around and then instantaneously switches character when they leave.

QUEEN BEE

"I'm in charge here—and don't you forget it!"

She rules the roost and commands attention. The center of the universe, everyone else must revolve around her. At the office she will often side with men against women and is the one that keeps other women from advancing. The office is her turf and she wants everyone to know it. The Queen Bee uses the politics of her network to roust out undesirables who do not accept her authority as she sees it.

At home, she can be the manipulating parent. When she is a "grandma," she still rules during visits to the family and grandchildren. She immediately takes over the house and begins making all the decisions for the family. If she is questioned or challenged, she pouts and acts deeply hurt.

Naming The Bitch

Other options for the Bitch appear in later chapters, but for now, on the next page, read the list of Bitches and in the appropriate blank space, note the frequency with which your bitches appear in your life, and describe the situations where you use her. (Use extra paper if needed).

And if you are feeling really courageous, ask a friend to help!

The Bitch	Qualities	Frequency of Use					Situations When You Still Use Her
		Used To	Never	Sometimes	Often	Always	
ICY MAIDEN	"I said there is nothing wrong ...(but you better know how I feel anyway)."	✓		✓			*Often with Gerard + Ma*

The Bitch	Qualities	Frequency of Use					Situations When You Still Use Her
		Used To	Never	Sometimes	Often	Always	
CASTRATING FEMALE	"Wait until I get through with this son of a bitch."			✓			With many a bit + with men I don't like + don't fancy
SHRIEKING WAR GODDESS	"Just what the hell do you mean by that!"	✓					With Edward + Martin
SEDUCTIVE MERMAID	"Come and get me . . . if you can."	✓		✓			With men I'm not attracted to when I get frightened
SACCHARINE BELLE	"Why honey, every-thing is just fine."		✓				
SUFFERING MARTYR	"Oh, that's alright . . . sigh . . . I'll do it anyway."	✓			✓	✓	With everyone I think I have to earn love from. In comp. w. Julie
PLEASING PASSIVE	"Whatever you say, dear."				✓		With Frank or someone I want to please.
SEDUCTIVE SIREN	"This one's a chal-lenge, but I will get him."				✓		On the rebound when I'm hurting + want reassurance. With other women
MOTHER SUPERIOR	"I told you so. If you had only lis-tened."			✓			When feeling inadequate. With Ma sometimes. On relationship w. Jam

The Bitch	Qualities	Frequency of Use					Situations When You Still Use Her
		Used To	Never	Sometimes	Often	Always	
ARMORED AMAZON	"I'm as good as any man...and you better believe it."						*With other BH teachers around Insight.*
GOLD DIGGER	"He meets all of my qualifications ...he's filthy rich."		✓				
BLACK WIDOW	"I like it when they squirm."		✓				
RESCUE ME	"Maybe he's the one."				✓		*Whenever I meet someone I'm attracted to. Hank Pete Frank. John*
ALL FEATHERS & NO BIRD	"Say what?"			✓			*V. consciously as a joke to get out of doing boring jobs*
WILTING BITCH	"I give up...I just can't handle it."					✓	*With girlfriends, + ma, in winter. Hopeless. When I'm lazy + want reassurance*
RECON— STRUCTED BITCH	"I can really get into that."			✓			*Still, hope I'm changing!*
BITTER BITCH	"After all I did for you and what did I get?"				✓		*With Gerard Frank tenk, when I'm not getting what I want*

The Bitch	Qualities	Frequency of Use					Situations When You Still Use Her
		Used To	Never	Sometimes	Often	Always	
NAGGING BITCH	"For God's sake Henry, put the top back on the tooth-paste."	✓				✓	With Edward + John. With Paul Hunting sort of jokingly on Team
TWO FACED BITCH	"Of course I will... (You bas-tard, I'll get you for this.")"			✓			When I feel I have no powerside with hmy In working situation
QUEEN BEE	"I'm in charge here and don't you forget it!"			✓			When IC ing. On staff with Mitzi + other women I don't respect.

BLOODY SERGGANT   Can't you see I'm bleeding to death + its all your fault? You Job.   ✓ When I'm wanting love + closeness + don't think I deserve it. If I think I've been rejected.

The Dragon Fight is the struggle
we have with ourselves when we reject
and rebel against our parents or strive to
emulate them. Either way there is a
fight. The Dragon Fight ends when we
are willing to accept our parents the way
they are, let ourselves be who we are,
and complete for ourselves
the job of parenting.

In order to heal the Dragon Fight,
we need to identify our patterns—
both the obvious and the hidden.
Once you identify your patterns,
then you will have the key to
understanding your own female-male
polarity and your relationship patterns.

CHAPTER 2

Ending the Dragon Fight

I remember as a child lying on a grassy bank on a hot summer evening, smelling the honeysuckle and gazing at the star-filled sky and wondering: Who am I? Where did I come from? Why was I born? Of all the possible places I could be, why am I living in this small town? And, why, of all the people on earth, am I with these parents?

Your parents were not perfect people but, they were the perfect parents for you. Whether you believe it now or not, I am convinced this is one of the most potentially healthy and healing attitudes you can develop about your parents.

Consider the possibility that, before you were born, a Divine Intelligence allowed you to choose your parents, and you specifically chose the ones you have. Whether this is true or not, or whether it can ever be proven scientifically or as a theological fact, doesn't matter. Just consider the possibility that you chose your parents because you recognized something about them that made them the perfect parents, the perfect teachers for whatever lessons, strengths, virtues, talents, or abilities you needed to develop in order to become whole in this life.

Every person, every situation we encounter in life presents us with an opportunity to learn something about ourselves. Life is a school, and we, by virtue of being alive on the planet, are automatically enrolled as students. In this School of Life our "teachers" are all the people in our lives who reflect or mirror back hidden qualities and aspects within us.

As teachers, their job is to help us to become more conscious of ourselves—because the requirement for graduation is, "Know thyself." The stronger our reaction to that person, the more intense our resistance or response to their lessons, the more valuable that teacher is.

Consider that your parents are important faculty members in this school. They have set up a curriculum for you and initiated lessons for your development and spiritual growth that you will be attempting to master for many years, if not for your entire life.

Parents act, mirror, exaggerate, and reflect whatever it is we need to learn. When we can stop reacting to those aspects of our parents that we don't like or approve of, and begin responding appropriately instead, then whatever they were doing to trigger us no longer has any power.

As I sat on that grassy bank, I thought, "I must be adopted." The notion was strangely comforting for me, an explanation my young mind could easily grasp. After all, my brothers and sister were dark, and I was fair and blonde. And certainly I had a different inner spirit.

"Mother, are you sure I am not adopted?" It was a question I asked more than once.

"Betty, really! Why do you keep asking that!" she'd reply with an air of peevishness. "Why would I adopt you, when I already had two children?"

Nevertheless, I wasn't convinced. I didn't feel I belonged. We weren't like a mother and daughter should be. And certainly, if I could have chosen my parents, I would have picked differently. Not that there wasn't love. There was. But, my father, as loving and nurturing as he was, was much too old-fashioned and restrictive for my spontaneous, adventurous nature. And mother. Well, that's where the battle really was. Sometimes a mother has one particular child that is her main challenge. I was definitely that one.

I wanted to take dance; she insisted on piano. I wanted to wear make-up; she thought I was too young. We battled over privacy, choice of friends, curfews, hair-style—everything! Or so it seemed. When I fell in love for the very first time—she refused to let Jimmy and me see each other. She didn't approve of him. He was from the wrong side of the tracks.

I was equally critical of her. Must she always wear heels—even when washing the clothes! Couldn't she, just once, be like other mothers and go to the grocery store in slacks? It's funny now, but in adolescence we tend to distort our view of ourselves and our parents.

On that grassy bank, I felt very alone and certain that I was the only girl who had these problems, the only one who struggled so intensely with her parents. The only one with a dragon to fight.

The Dragon Fight

In myths and fairytales, one of the archetypal tasks of the hero—or heroine—is to slay a dragon. The dragon is usually a ferocious, fire-breathing monster, big and powerful, often guarding a treasure, and always making people cower in fear. And thus, keeping them from ex-periencing and expressing life fully.

Art therapist Joan Kellogg in her book, *Mandala: Path of Beauty* uses the term "Dragon Fight" to describe the age-old conflict that children have in establishing their own identities. The dragon is the symbol for the parents, and the fight begins early in life. At the heart of the Dragon Fight is the issue of our own individuality—

our own ability to become who we really are.

* * *

The Dragon Fight is the struggle we
have with ourselves when we reject and rebel
against our parents—or strive to emulate
them. Either way, there is a fight.

The Dragon Fight ends when we are willing to let our parents be who they are and
when we can let ourselves be who we are and
complete for ourselves the job of parenting.

* * *

Throughout our most formative and dependent
years, our mother and father are the only models we
have of the world. They gave us our first ideas of who we
are and what it means to be male and female, and they
provide us with the primary role models for our masculine and feminine selves. And by "mother" and "father,"
I don't necessarily mean the biological parents. The
terms can refer to the primary people, who, in our early
lives, gave us ideas of what it means to be male or
female. They could be a grandparent, an aunt or uncle,
or any other important adult.

The mother and the father figures inform us if
we are "naughty" or "nice." We learn from them what
it takes to be a good girl and whether we will ever
achieve it.

The moment we start to feel that our parents aren't
giving us all that we need to feel "all right" about ourselves, the battles begin. If we feel disappointed or
cheated in life because of the parents we have, we may
cry, "Why was I born to them!" And then, because we
feel critical and resentful—or ashamed and embarrassed—we reject them and rebel by becoming the
opposite of everything they stand for. Or, if we are afraid

that they are disappointed in us or that we can never measure up to their expectations, we will strive to emulate them, making ourselves over in their image in order to gain acceptance and approval. Either way there is a fight, because we have not differentiated ourselves and accepted who we are. We begin to feel unloved and insecure, and then we start blaming them for our own lack of self-worth.

When this happens, we are fighting dragons. The relationship with our parents stops developing, and we may remain the fearful child, the rebellious daughter, or the blaming adolescent for life.

Though the Dragon Fight is about parents, we don't always fight it out with our parents. Whatever has been unresolved with our parents carries over into other relationships. Someone else may be playing the mother role, or the father figure for us—husband, lover, children, bosses, teachers, the bus driver, or the sales clerk. Whatever we wanted and didn't get from our parents, we will try to get from them.

Healing can take place whether there is a direct relationship with the parents or not. You are still in a relationship with them whether they are thousands of miles apart, no longer living, or if you haven't made contact since childhood. You still carry your relationship inside you, and that relationship colors your outlook in every area of your life. It effects the way you look at yourself, the way you feel about your own femininity and masculinity, and all your relationships, including your relationship to the Source of Life, the Spirit within you.

During my years of counseling, one of the saddest things was watching seventy and eighty-year-old cancer patients crying on their deathbeds over an unresolved relationship with their parents. This need is so deep that after a lifetime of the Dragon Fight, there is a last attempt to end it. Outward battle or inner struggle, the fight goes on until the dragon is slain.

The Parent Picture

On a sheet of paper, using colored pencils, crayons, or markers, draw your mother and father. Draw them the way you see them—as people, not as symbols. In other words, don't make your parent a star or a tree or a rainbow, but a person.

It doesn't matter if you know how to draw or not—what matters is that you attempt to picture your parents as close as you can to the way you see them—and the pictures are almost always more accurate than anything you can get with your camera! The mind is often deceptive, and we can fool ourselves about our real feelings. Through spontaneous or impromptu drawings, the unconscious expresses itself and often communicates more clearly than our rational process.

The key to this exercise is to be spontaneous. As you draw, allow your feelings to express themselves.

Complete your drawing before turning to the next sections. Reading ahead may alter your experience.

What The Parent Picture Means

It's Really You

While your Parent Picture is about your parents, everything that you draw is really about yourself. We will go into this in greater detail later in this chapter. The Parent Picture gives information in four specific areas:

1. How you see your parents

In order to reconcile, resolve, and break out of old patterns, you need to be honest about your feelings toward your parents, to understand the interaction you

had with each parent, and to understand the relationship they had with each other.

2. Your relationship patterns

Though the Dragon Fight is about parents, we don't
always fight it out with them in particular. Whatever is
not resolved with our parents we project onto others. We
usually attract the same or opposite patterns in our
"significant other" relationships than the one our parents
had. Women will be like the mother and draw "father"
as a partner (or the opposite match, which means we
are still working with the same issue). The more dysfunctional the pattern, the more desperate the attempt
to recreate the same pattern. It is usually a misplaced
effort to heal the original pattern.

3. Your female-male balance

The figures in your Parent Picture represent your
feminine-masculine qualities and how integrated and
balanced they are. The following is a guideline for
delineating these feminine and masculine qualities.

FEMININE	MASCULINE
Gentle	Strong
Right-Brain	Left-Brain
Feelings	Logic
Emotions	Reasoning
Receptive	Assertive
Spontaneous	Organized
Nurturing	Protective
Scattered	Disciplined
Wisdom	Knowledge
Vulnerable	Rigid
Understanding	Judgment
Moon	Sun
Unconscious	Conscious
Cold	Hot

Introverted	Extroverted
Intuitive	Pragmatic
Form	Force
Spatial	Linear

4. What you need to do in parenting—take responsibility for—yourself. For example:

Is the picture too rigid?
　　　You need more flexibility.

A parent has no feet.
　　　You need more roots, grounding.

Is the picture too serious?
　　　Lighten up, you need to laugh.

It takes training and intuition to interpret all the subtleties of the drawings, and there are few, if any, hard-and-fast rules about the various meanings of the different elements of any drawing. However, the following are offered as guidelines so that you can gain insight into your parent-child relationship and into yourself through your drawing.

Remember, choice of color and color combinations is also significant and reveals other insights for interpretation. However, color interpretation is a complex and intricate art in itself, and will be dealt with in more detail in a future book.

Interpreting Your Drawing: Things To Look For

Mood

What is the overall mood of your parents?

Are they somber, rigid, open? Is that how you express yourself?

Roles

A. Take your drawing and crease it down the middle. Usually the mother is on the left and the father is on the right. If they are reversed, what does this tell you about who played which role in your life?

Did "male" and "female" get switched for you?

Do you attract "masculine" women or "feminine" men?

B. Which of your parents dominates?

If one of the parents is noticeably weak, who in your life plays that role for you now? (For example, women who draw a small or insignificant father figure will usually attract extremes—either very weak men or overbearing "macho" types—in their lives).

Is that part within you (the masculine side, the feminine side) underdeveloped?

C. How close or separated are your parents from each other? Are they touching or are they distant?

What does the picture say about how you relate to significant men/women in your life now?

How integrated are your male and female aspects?

Body Language

A. How much of your parents did you draw? (Just the head, the head and shoulders, etc.) How well do you know your parents? How well do you know yourself?

B. What part of their bodies has the most focus? Look for any part of the body that stands out. What parts of the body are emphasized and which parts are weak or undeveloped? How accurate are your drawings? (If your father was slim, did you draw him fat? If your mother was flat chested, did you draw her with a bosom? *etc.*)

Look for symbolic rather than literal interpretations of the body. If you drew your father with no ears, that may mean that you felt he never "heard" you. If your mother has an ample bosom, you may have felt her to be very nurturing.

Symbols And Their Common Associations

Clenched Jaw

Unexpressed feelings, overly self-controlled.

Ears

Unless covered with long hair, they should be present. If they are missing, it could indicate whether you felt listened to or not.

Hair

Hair represents thoughts. Is the hair wild, controlled, free, tight?

Eyes

Eyes represent how you see things. What are the feelings, the expression conveyed through the eyes?

The rounder the eyes, the more love or warmth is suggested. Deep set eyes suggest a critical thinker.

Mouth

The mouth symbolizes communication. Full lips usually indicate someone who likes to communicate.

Thin, tight lips suggest anger, tensions, feelings that have been held in, or thoughts that want to be expressed.

Neck

This is the connector between the mind and emotions, or the head and the heart. Often the neck will be overlooked, or covered with clothing, scarves, bands, or necklaces. This suggests a restriction in that area, i.e., that feelings are cut off from the rest of the body. This usually is found with very mental people who are out of touch with their feelings. The neck is also the part of the body that is often associated with will, i.e., "stiff-necked."

Shoulders

Burdens are carried in the shoulders. Hunched up shoulders can indicate fear. Broad shoulders: someone who "shoulders" responsibilities, who is confident, trustworthy.

Arms

Ability to express, to reach out. Are the arms rigid, hands in pockets, locked behind the body? This could indicate the parent was not able to give or be available to you.

Elbows

A graceful bend to the elbows suggests flexibility, adaptability; stiffness suggests a rigidity of self-expression.

Torso

This part of the body reflects the sense of self. A slumping position indicates lack of self worth. A protruding or overly large torso, in proportion to the rest of the body, indicates an overbearing nature, or someone who is "puffed up" with self.

Bosom

This indicates the ability to be warm and nurturing. Notice whether you drew your mother with large breasts, though in real life she may have very small breasts. A very flat chest usually indicates unwillingness to be a woman; a desire to remain protected as a little girl rather than to be grown up.

Solar Plexus

The solar plexus is the area of the adrenals, the seat of our emotions. If there is a lot of emphasis in this area in the drawing, it can indicate emotional issues that need to be worked through, or emotions that need to be expressed. Look particularly for tight or dominant belts. This can suggest repressed sexuality, a condition of keeping everything tight and under control.

Legs

Legs are what we stand on, and represent foundation and support. Look to see whether legs are out of proportion to the rest of the body (too large or too small).

Weak, underdeveloped legs indicate a weak foundation.

Sluggish legs denote difficulty in initiating action.

Thick or overly muscular legs reflect brute force.

Feet

Feet give us balance. They represent physical or psychological grounding. Look to see if the feet are flat on the ground. A drawing on tiptoes or with off-balanced feet indicate a hard time making contact physically or psychologically with life. These people tend to be dreamers. Feet that do not touch the ground or base of the picture show a person who is not grounded— up in the air.

What direction are the feet pointing (away from or toward the male or female figures)?

Parent Picture Reflections

1. What does your drawing tell you about how you see your parents?

2. How does this picture reflect your most significant female/male relationship patterns (past or present)? Are they similar, the same, opposite? Does it represent an earlier pattern, but one you have moved beyond?

3. The next level is to internalize your drawing. Remember, the mother and father you drew also relates to your feminine/masculine aspects.

Now look at your drawing as a picture of yourself. What does it suggest about your male and female sides? Which side looks stronger, happier, underdeveloped, weak, dominant, etc.?

4. What does your picture suggest about what you need to do for yourself in order to become more balanced and whole?

Parenting Yourself

Write in the spaces below. Use extra paper if necessary.

1. What didn't your parents do for you?

2. Why didn't they do it?

3. What do you wish they had done?

4. What would you have gotten from it?

After answering these questions, remind yourself that *your parents have done their job.* Whatever was not done by them is now up to you to complete for yourself.

5. How can you complete the job of parenting yourself now?

Creating Our Parents

We create our parents! It is a fact. None of us have the same parents we were born to. Of course, we have the same biological parents. That can't be changed. But the mother, the father you have today are the ones that you created as a result of your experiences with them.

To illustrate, take a moment and imagine that you and your parents are sitting down together at a large table. You have a sheet of paper in front of you that says: "Describe your parents' three most outstanding traits." In front of your parents are two sheets, and they say: "Describe your three most outstanding traits." You take a few moments to reflect, recalling past experiences and your thoughts and feelings about them. You look across the table and see your parents reflecting also. And as you watch them taking these few moments to examine themselves, the traits you associate with them come clearly to your mind, and you begin to write.

What are the three things that you put on your list? Are they the same ones you would have described them with when you were five years old? When you were a teenager? Five years ago? Six months ago? Will those same traits be the ones you will see in them five years from now?

Now take a few moments and visualize yourself back in that room with your parents. What did they write on their list? How do you think they described themselves? Is their list the same as yours? Or do they see themselves differently than you do?

Who are your parents? The ones you made up? Or, are they who they think they are? Or, could it be that who they really are is beyond both your and their perception?

One thing is clear. We all have beliefs and opinions about our mothers and fathers, and these come out of our experience with them. Our relationship with our parents is colored by these beliefs and opinions. And beliefs can be changed. Therefore our experiences— past, present, and future—can all be changed. That is part of the magic we have—the power to transform.

No Two Parents Are The Same!

Several years ago, two sisters took the *Emerging Woman* seminar in Washington, D.C. When it came time for the "Parent Picture," the results were astounding!

Marlene, the older sister, using dark colors, drew her father as austere and remote. Everything about her drawing suggested her father was closed and aloof. His hands were in his pockets, his head was turned away, and there was a significant space separating the two figures. On the other hand, Meryl, the younger sister, drew a light, bright, cheerful man with a smile on his face with his arms opened invitingly at his side. Could this be the same person?

The portraits of their mother were equally diverse. Marlene drew her mother with light, bright colors. She was attractive, well proportioned, and projected a warm and sunny disposition—a born nurturer. Meryl pictured her mother as a puffy, bloated, tight-lipped woman, glowering through tense, slit eyes with her hands on her hips in a rigid and judgmental posture. A frightening harridan!

No drawings of parents are ever alike. Children in the same family will all have different experiences and relationships with the same set of parents, as their parents will with them. But with Marlene and Meryl, the differences were almost unbelievable. The two pictures were so totally dissimilar that it would be impossible to guess that they represented the same set of parents!

Marlene's experience with her parents was totally different than Meryl's. For Marlene, the mother was the available one, warm, and touchable. For Meryl, it was the father. Same parents—different realities.

Hidden Dragons:
The Saint-Sinner Syndrome

Some of the dragons we face are obvious ones. We are aware of which parent and which issues within us are raised as we interact with that parent. We are conscious of our buttons being pushed, are aware of how and when we react, and have insights into how and in what way they mirror us. And even if we have not totally ended our Dragon Fight, we are well on our way just by virtue of being conscious of our own process, by resisting the urge to blame, and by taking sole responsibility for ending the fight.

The real challenge comes, though, when the dragon is more disguised. These are the hidden dragons. Not only are the lessons camouflaged, but often we don't even see which parent is our real dragon.

* * *

The parent that we are sure we have the issues with is often not that one. We are hiding from the real dragon.

* * *

The saint-sinner syndrome occurs when we are determined to overvalue one parent and to undervalue another. As long as we see one parent as saint and the other as sinner, madonna or whore, king or bum, there is a corresponding imbalance within ourselves, and we will tend to attract relationships in which we will not be able to see the other person clearly.

Mother, Is It You?

At an Emerging Woman seminar in London, Margaret assumed that her major conflict was with her alcoholic and abusive father. He was the obvious dragon.

During the course of the weekend, she realized that her major issue was not with her father but with her mother whom she blamed and resented for not protecting her from him. With her mother she had her deepest and most buried feelings of distrust!

As Margaret continued exploring her own feelings and taking a closer look at her own patterns, she confronted an alarming truth. Like her mother, she could not stand up for herself. She failed to be firm and clear. And she avoided taking positive steps or making direct, clear communications to meet unpleasant situations for fear of losing the love of those she held dear. In many ways, she was just like her mother!

As she began to understand herself, Margaret began to understand her mother. Compassion replaced recrimination. Margaret gained new strength, a new sense of self-worth, and the potential for new directions in her life. She had unearthed the gold that could enrich her life.

At this point, Margaret forgave her mother, releasing her from further blame. As her final step, Margaret pledged to let go of the need to please others at the cost of her own integrity and to empower herself through right action.

There is an interesting paradox that accompanies the saint-sinner syndrome. Usually the parent that we consider to be the sinner holds the key to our greatest challenge. Whatever triggers us the most, about that parent, does so because we are either afraid that underneath we are just like them or we haven't developed any of that quality and probably need some of it. Usually we avoid that energy and that part of ourselves. It remains a disowned part. The resolution of the paradox comes when we can strike a balance between possessing none of that quality and possessing it to an extreme.

We know we have reached that balance when we use that energy appropriately.

Sandra's Story

Sandra's father was overbearing, difficult, angry, and authoritarian. His communications were direct and forceful. At the dinner table she remembers being told in abusive language, "Shut up and eat your dinner." Sandra avoided problems with her father by imitating her mother's behavior: being quiet and staying out of his way. Mother was mild-mannered, non-confrontational, and did everything nice for her family—but in her quiet way, she made it obvious she was a Suffering Martyr. To Sandra, mother was the saint and daddy was the sinner.

When she married, she re-enacted the same patterns as her mother, playing the nice, sweet, Pleasing Passive to an overbearing, angry male. After many years, her husband walked out on her. Sandra was bitter about men. Self-righteous about her plight, she wondered why she had to suffer so much and why her life was so difficult. The martyr pattern was deeply ingrained.

Sandra was in no hurry to replace her husband. The years passed and she was comfortable in a nurturing role with men and chose to keep her relationships on a friendship basis. A deep interest in spirituality, religion, and philosophical concepts filled the void for her. Her energy went to the Father God.

In her fifties, life presented Sandra with a difficult challenge. Her ailing mother came to live with her. She was bedridden and required constant care. The tension and stress of dealing with her mother's nursing care and confinement began to take its toll on Sandra. Working all day at a full-time job and then coming home to, in essence, another full-time commitment was wearing physically and emotionally. Meanwhile, her mother was ridden with pain and often overcome with depression.

"Can you turn me again? Is there something else to eat other than this? I need something else to drink. The light is too bright. Turn it down." The needs seemed endless. Sandra's attitude toward her mother changed. She no longer saw her as the saint; she wearied of her complaints. Much to her surprise, Sandra found herself responding to her mother in a style very similar to that of the father. There *was* some redeeming quality to his insistence on directness. What a revelation! Sandra discovered she had to set limits for her own time and for what she could and could not do, even though she may want to, for her mother. She was forced to develop the positive male within herself. Her challenge was to communicate with the directness of the father but to avoid the harsh negative tone.

Now that Sandra sees the value of her father (he dealt directly rather than being passive/aggressive), she is less inhibited and more open and honest in her communications. She can stop being a Suffering Martyr and a Pleasing Passive. And her mother has to come off her pedestal. Though she nurtured well, she wasn't direct and didn't know how to stand up for herself!

Often we discover, as did Sandra, that our greatest strength comes once we understand the parent with whom we had our greatest challenge! And as Sandra can see the value of not just one, but both parents, she can come more into balance within herself.

Healing the Dragon Fight

When I lay on that grassy bank as a little child, wondering why I had been placed in that family, I was sure that the real dragon to fight was my mother. But many years later, an incident occurred which jolted me into a new awareness.

It was when David, my older son, was just a toddler. I took him "home" to Front Royal to visit. One evening, my mother offered to put David to bed and from the next room I could hear her singing a lullaby. The words, the cadences, the inflections were identical to the way I sang the same song. The same caring and tenderness I felt for little David was in her voice. And I wondered how could I ever have thought we were so unlike each other. How could I have missed this part of her?

It took many years to understand that from her I had gained enormous strength, a sense of independence and individuality, and I could see her as dynamic, talented, and warm. As I have claimed my own identity and power, I am able to give hers back to her. She can be who she is, and so can I.

The truth is we can end the dragon fight anytime we want.

It requires only three things:

1. Accept that our parents were not perfect people, but they were the perfect parents for us. They gave us the exact challenges we needed to become whole women.

2. Next, we must give our parents back to our parents. Let them be who they are. They can never be real people as long as we hold on to our ideas, beliefs, and opinions about who or how we want them to be, or how they should be, or could have been. When we can accept them as they really are—they no longer have to be the way we want them to be, and we both are free.

3. Finally, to end the Dragon Fight we must take responsibility for parenting and loving ourselves. Whatever our parents didn't do for us, we have to do for ourselves. It is that simple.

No More Tears

Leslie was a forty-year-old woman who came for counseling after a seminar in Houston. Her clothes were colorless and drab, and she was distant and removed from her feelings. Through the seminar, I was already aware of some of the issues in her life. Leslie's mother had died when she was three, and that had created a gap in her life that nothing seemed to fill. Thirty-seven years later, she was still grieving the loss of her mother and blaming her stepmother. She experienced her step-mother as harsh and uncaring and faulted her for the lack of love and nurturing in her life.

At that time, I sometimes included therapeutic massage in my sessions. Leslie was on the massage table, and as the session came to a close, I felt a sudden impulse to wrap her in the blanket in a particular way. As I folded the cover around her, I said, "No more tears, Leslie. No more tears." The words seemed to flow from me without having to think them, and tears began flooding down her face. My spontaneous gesture of empathy and caring connected Leslie with a memory of her mother tucking her in bed, and she shook with a power-ful release of pent-up emotion. From the depths of her being, she wailed and sobbed as feelings of loss and sad-ness came spilling out. And then, at last, she sighed a sigh of acceptance. It was finished. It was time now for living.

In subsequent sessions, Leslie released more of her pain and accepted the responsibility for parenting her-self. She began to do all the pampering and nurturing of herself that she had yearned for her mother to do. She became her own loving mother valuing her thoughts and feelings. She started to love her body, pay attention to her appearance, indulge in long, hot soaking baths, and have massages. For the first time in her life, shop-ping and picking out colorful and attractive clothing for herself was fun, not a chore. Her inner metamorphosis was complete when, at a party, a young man told her, "You are a striking and beautiful woman." She was delightfully shocked to discover that others saw her that way.

Cold, Rigid And Dressed In Black

When I met Lynn, she was preparing to die. She was an attractive thirty-five-year-old woman, with a wonderfully supportive husband and three children. And she was dying from cancer. Two years before she had had a mastectomy and the metastasis had spread throughout her body. In the face of death, Lynn's attitude was unusually positive. She had carefully put her life in order, assuring as smooth a transition for herself and her family as possible. Everything in her life was organized, and she faced the prognosis bravely, with great courage.

When our counseling sessions began, there was only one thing left unfinished—her relationship with her mother, and that concerned her deeply. As our sessions unfolded, I could hardly believe that such a woman existed—until I actually met her. And then I could see she was exactly as Lynn described her—cold, rigid, severe, no touching, no show of any feeling. Standing silently in the hospital room in her long black coat with her hair chopped ragged and close to her head, it was impossible to imagine her as a mother. She seemed more like a grim prison warden.

In one session, Lynn remembered a painful childhood experience that was so humiliating and traumatic for her that it literally chilled me as she relived it.

"I was six years old," she said. "I had a new dress on, and I got it wet. I was playing by the stream, and I wasn't supposed to play there. When my mother found me there, she began screaming and yelling about the dress—and what a bad girl I was!" Lynn paused and took a deep breath. It was obvious the pain of this experience was deeply imbedded in her soul.

"And then she started to yank and pull me. And the next thing I knew she had a rope. She was still yelling and shouting at me about ruining the dress. And then she pushed me against a tree and tied me to it." Lynn bit her lip and tried to hold back her tears. She started to cry.

"And she left me there," she said. I could hear the frightened child in her voice, still trembling, bewildered, and alone.

The painful memories had to be healed. So much of herself was invested in those early wounds. Whatever part of us that is caught in the past, cannot live in the present.

The next day, I took Lynn through a guided visualization experience. To heal those early childhood memories, it was important to take her back to that same time period and recreate the experience and transform it.

She lay quietly before me. Her eyes were closed, and she was breathing rhythmically while soft, soothing music played in the background. I gave a suggestion to go back in time, to when she was six years old, and this time there would be a strong, loving person there to help her.

Lynn found herself tied to the tree again, feeling alone and terrified.

"Is there anyone there to help you?" I asked.

She paused.

"Yes," she murmured, "Jesus." Her voice was calm and even. "Jesus is coming down the path to help me." Lynn was a woman of great faith, and I knew, from other conversations, that Jesus was someone she trusted.

"What is He doing now?" I asked.

"He is walking toward me." She smiled. "And how

he is untying the rope. There, now the rope is gone."

"What do you feel now?"

"I'm not afraid anymore. I feel totally loved, filled." Suddenly her face relaxed totally and she was silent.

I stopped, careful not to intrude upon this moment, allowing the inner experience to unfold. Her face tensed slightly.

"What is happening now?"

"I see my mother. She's dressed in black. She looks angry. I feel afraid."

"Don't stop now, Lynn. Go on. What's happening now?"

"Jesus has me by the hand, and we're walking toward my mother. I'm not afraid. Now we're standing together in a circle. We're all holding hands. My mother is smiling, and so is Jesus."

Lynn grew silent again, her inner gaze fixed upon that scene of love and reconciliation. She opened her eyes and smiled.

"My mother didn't know how to be a mother." There wasn't a trace of criticism, pain, or judgment in her voice. "When we were standing in the circle, holding hands with Jesus, I could feel how scared and frustrated being a parent made her. It was something she wasn't ever very good at."

For the next few days, Lynn practiced visualizing a reconciliation with her mother. She had healed the past, and now she wanted to heal the present. In her mind, she visualized herself sitting in her rocking chair in her front room, and her mother coming toward her, and both of them embracing. She practiced this visualization over and over again—until it became a living experience.

Two weeks after the guided imagery session she and her mother were reconciled. "For the first time in my life, my mother actually reached out and hugged me," Lynn told me. "She actually had tears in her eyes.

We both cried together."

Four months later, Lynn died. She died in her sleep, in peace. She was a powerful teacher for me.

Fears To Pass Through:
The Death Of My Father

My father was eighty-five years old when he died of cancer. He had always been an energetic, positive, vibrant man. His diagnosis was not easy for him. But the same humor, iron will, and absolute honesty with which he had always approached life stayed with him during his illness.

Several months before he died, I had a short but vivid dream that awakened me in the middle of the night. In the dream, my father was scratching his skin and pulling his hair.

In real life, my father had no hair. He had been bald all my life. The dream had a symbolic message for me. My father (my male side) was disturbed. Scratching skin indicated things bothering me (getting under my skin), and the hair pulling was thoughts I wanted to release. Dreams are first and foremost about the self. In this dream, though, I knew my father was in a similar dilemma. It was an intense dream; it seemed an urgent call for help. The next morning, I cancelled all my appointments and made the five-hour drive back to Front Royal.

Five hours is a long time to drive, and I did some serious soul-searching along the way. My father was the parent I always wanted to emulate. He was warm, generous, and wise. And, although we didn't always agree, I valued his high ideals and integrity. His way of life was honorable and respectful. It was what I was striving for in my own way.

With my father, there were no secrets. He was

frank, open, and clear. And he was facing his illness, as he had his life, with directness and honesty. He had no illusions. He knew his cancer was terminal, and he had chosen to spend his last days at home, with his family, and to die in his own bed.

As I drove, knowing he had only a short time left, I had no doubts about the bond between us. Our love for each other was strong and clear. But what wasn't clear was his understanding and acceptance of my divorce. The thought of his leaving without this sensitive issue being resolved was painful. I had talked with him about it, but there was a lot I hadn't shared with him, a lot I had left unsaid.

My father didn't believe in divorce. Marriages were forever, regardless. Although he was a staunch Baptist, to me, he was like a wise and benevolent rabbi, a kind but firm man of the law. I knew he had suffered a great deal over my decision to divorce. Would he accept me as a divorced woman who chooses for herself, with her own reasons for dissolving the marriage bonds? I knew he wanted to understand my reasons. But it was difficult for me. It required me to voice things that were hard to say. If I couldn't be honest and he died not totally at peace with me, how would I feel? With this cloud still over us, how would he feel? Could I trust myself to express my views confidently and directly, still valuing my decisions if my father didn't approve—even on his deathbed? Or would I hold back and become the Pleasing Passive even now?

"Betty, be yourself." My father's counsel to me had always been wise and simple. "Be natural, know your heart." Those words have always been a source of strength for me. In myths, the dragon slayer is the one who knows himself, trusts his own ability, and confronts the task—not by comparing his strength to the strength of the dragon, but by attuning himself to that source of life and power within. As I drove up to the house, my prayer was that I would be guided by love, not fear.

There were some awkward moments at first. I was strained and overcautious, and, at times, I found myself falling into my familiar pattern of holding back. My deepest, heart-felt desire was to say all I needed to say, and I sensed I would never have an opportunity with my father like this again. The love was stronger than my fears. The nervousness quickly faded, and soon I began sharing intimately and fully.

We spent four days together. We laughed. We talked. We cried. Many issues were healed during those hours together, both in my life and his. At times the parent-child role reversed. I was the mother and he, the son; I became the teacher and he, the student. I was no longer just a daughter, but a friend, a loved one—a whole person. In those hours together, he shared more about himself and his understanding of life than I had ever imagined.

On the last day we were together, I sat in the room, watching him as he dozed. Suddenly, I felt the urge to go over and put my hands all over his face and that wonderful, shiny bald head. I stood there, touched to the core, pouring out all the deep love I had for him. He awoke, and with misty eyes and a smile, he looked up at me and said, "We really do love each other, don't we?" At the end of those four days, when I left my father, I knew he was at peace. And so was I.

The feelings had been deep, and there were moments of great sadness. But as I drove back to Virginia Beach, the sadness didn't touch me, not now. There was too much to be thankful for, too much to appreciate: the dream that had called me to him, the absolute clarity and conviction I had felt welling up within me to be with him, and then the strength, the love—to speak, to communicate from the heart. As father and daughter, and as soul to soul, we had experienced and explored new depths and intimacy with each other.

I was all I could be to him, and he had shared himself fully with me. It was a moment of Life, not death, for both of us.

A few days later, my mother telephoned to say my father's cancer had advanced. Any fleeting hope of a remission was gone. The cancer had spread all through his body. His last remaining strength was gone. He was now too weak to speak. Those wonderful, comforting words of this great man would be no more. I sat down and wept. The tears were bitter sweet.

Yes, there had been fears to pass through. Both he and I were making transitions, and the love and support we had given one another had prepared us to step into that Unknown that lay ahead in his life and mine.

Healing The Relationship With Your Parents

(Allow 10-15 minutes or longer)

Begin by playing soothing, relaxing music. Lie down or sit with your spine erect. Take a few breaths, breathing in peace, relaxation, stillness, and breathing out tension, stress, negativity. Let your breathing be rhythmical and easy.

Reverie

Find yourself in a meadow—move and feel the earth under your bare feet. Feel the texture of the grass as you walk. Become aware of the presence of life all around you, the sounds of animals, the songs of birds, the music of the breeze blowing gently through the trees, the splash of water in a nearby brook. It is twilight.

Soft light slants across the meadow.

Move to a clearing in the meadow. Off to the side there is a clump of trees. As you stand there in the clearing, your mother and father step out from the trees. Look at them curiously.

Who are these people?

(Pause)

Now your mother steps forward. Be aware of the relationship you had with her. What was it like? Be aware of what you feel—not what you were supposed to feel. It doesn't matter that everybody says that you are supposed to love your mother. If you did, you did. And if you don't, you don't.

Do you love her? Do you not love her? Whatever you feel is all right.

What is it you want to say to her now? Say all those things you've never said. Communicate them non-verbally. If you need to forgive, forgive. If you need to be angry, be angry. If you want to tell her she did a good job, say so. Say all the things that you need to say.

(Long pause)

Now look closely at this woman. Be aware of her humanness. Be aware that she was never trained to be your mother. Imagine what it was like for her to have you as her daughter. Look into her eyes and be aware that this woman did all she knew to do.

Understand as much as you can about her at this moment. Accept what you can. Ask yourself, what do I need to do to heal this relationship?

Now she steps back, and your father steps forward.

Be aware of the relationship you had with him. What was it like? Be aware of what you feel as he steps forward—not what you were supposed to feel. Do you love him? Do you not love him? Whatever you feel is all right. It doesn't matter that everybody says that you are supposed to love your father. If you did, you did. And if you don't, you don't.

What is it you want to say to him right now? Say all those things you've never said. Communicate them non-verbally. If you need to forgive him, forgive. If you need to be angry, be angry. If you want to tell him he was great, tell him. Say all the things that you need to say. Experience it, and get finished with it.

(Pause)

Now look closely at this man. Be aware of his humanness. Be aware that he was never trained to be your father. Imagine what it was like for him to have you as his daughter. Look into his eyes and be aware that this man did all he knew to do.

Understand as much as you can about him at this moment. Accept what you can. Ask yourself, what do I need to do to heal this relationship?

(Pause)

Now he steps back and joins your mother. Watch them as they step back into the grove of trees.

Turn and leave the clearing. Walk across the meadow. Be aware that you can come to this meadow as often as you like to be with your parents.

Notice now the day is nearly over. The last bit of light fades from the sky. Slowly bring the experience to a close.

Leave the meadow. Bring your attention back to

your body and to the room you are in. Be with your feelings for a moment...start to stretch your body... breathe deeply...move...come back refreshed.

NOTE:

For best and most lasting results, write out your experience in a journal, or discuss your feelings with your partner or support group. By sharing and communicating, we reinforce the experience.

The experience should be repeated many times. Do it as often as you feel necessary until the relationship is healed.

Four Parent Picture Examples

The commentary on these four Parent Pictures will help you better assess your own drawing.

The Pleasing Passive

• Irene sees her mother as a little girl, a Pleasing Passive. Note the woman's feet pointing toward the man, the outstretched hand with the flowers, and the pubescent body (no curves, no bosom, no shape in the legs).

• The tight arms, chains, choker on the neck and the "buttoned up" front suggest the woman feels a prisoner by her self-assigned role, but is determined to stay pleasing and pretty all the while.

• The father appears youthful and immature. The broad shoulders, thick arms and heavy hands suggest a lot of power. Notice the thick belt over an out-of-proportion groin area—strong sexual energy and a difficult task in controlling it. His feet are pointing away from the female, indicating his direction is away from hers, and she is in pursuit of him.

• As a result of her early conditioning, Irene, like so many women, is unsure about male energy. When men are dominating, angry, forceful, she confuses that with power because it gets results. She identifies with the mother, and is overwhelmed when this assertive, forceful male energy is directed at her. Irene has a lot of underlying terror about men and her inability to stand up to them and to express herself. To "keep things nice," she stays a Pleasing Passive, not a mature, real woman.

• As long as she looks outside of herself, to the men in her life, for approval, she will never have it. What she is reaching out for so desperately in the picture is her own positive male self.

The Stronger Of The Two

- So much about Vivian's perception of her parents is communicated just by the placement of the figures on the page. The father is turned sideview and the mother's gaze is turned away from him.

- Certainly, Vivian considers her mother the stronger of the two. She has inner serenity, an inner confidence, and graceful beauty that makes her a most compelling woman. She appears self-contained as though she has neither the need nor the desire for the man to fulfill her. Though the copy of the drawing is only in black and white, in the original drawing, the mother is arrayed in beautiful and harmonious colors, symbolizing the colorful and interesting nature of this woman. She is no doubt artistic, with a keen aesthetic sense.

- On the other hand, the father is drawn in weak, vague, nondescript colors. He is a very feminine man, and Vivian perceives him as needing to be taken care of by the stronger woman. He is sensitive and soft, a "Peter Pan" or "flying boy" who has not cultivated his own sense of self-direction and waits for the woman to wake him up. The side-view, reflecting partial understanding, suggests Vivian does not know this man well.

- Vivian identifies with the mother. As an adult, her attractions and affection are directed toward women. She feels secure with women, particularly with older women who display the same inner strength that she so admired in her mother.

- The drawing indicates that Vivian wants to forget about her father and men in general. That is all the more reason she needs to deal with them. There may be an earlier incident that she is trying to blot out. It would be helpful to open and explore early memories and experiences with her father. Also, by developing male friendships (open communication, understanding, mutual respect), Vivian could learn to value men much more.

Everything In Its Place

• This picture could have been drawn by many individuals, especially those who had the similar pre-1950s family. In this scenario, which was common in that generation, the father was "higher" and the mother was "lower."

• Notice that carefully-drawn, clear line that the mother stands on and the father steps over. This is a traditional family structure and there is a sense of security knowing that meals are regular, bed time is a special ritual, daddy comes home for dinner, and there is always milk money in the school lunchbox. There is a sense of keeping everything nice. Everything fits into its own pigeon-hole. And, as with all constructs, this system possesses its strengths and weaknesses.

• Jeanette's father is depicted as strong, reliable, responsible, capable. The pitchfork and shovel in his hand gives him a sense of a strong work ethic. There is a feeling that this man is direct and orderly. He is the strong one in the family and definitely wields the power. Notice that he is the only one in the picture with a mouth, emphasizing that he is the voice for the family. The mother also fits the traditional role model of that time. She is nurturing, hard-working, and supportive. Notice that she stands on the line. She is secure with her position and knows not to cross into his territory.

• Jeanette places herself between the two parents, closer to the mother. And the mother's hand rests gently on her shoulder. It would seem that she would tend to model herself after her mother and attempt to re-enact the same scenario in her marriage. Jeanette is slightly "off the line" but has not ventured forward yet. She too has work to do. The work ethic runs deep and a lot of her value will be determined according to what she does and not who she is.

• All appears in order, except for the heavy lines beneath the figures. This indicates there is a lot underneath that is not explored or dealt with yet. There is a tight lid on things—and that lid is not to be taken off.

• Because of Jeanette's rigid patterning, her tendency would be to make life the way it should be rather than how it is. Her challenge and break-through

came with a daughter who helped her with these barriers. Her daughter did not fit the mold. And during the
rebellious period, she was sexually promiscuous and
was a political activist. This forced her mother out of conservative thinking. Either we make changes gracefully or
life has a way of forcing our hand. Often we need
extremes to bring us out of our shells.

The Jaded Eye

• When people draw only a face, and in this case
with only one feature, the distorted view indicates how
little the child knows the parent. Leah sees her father as
a real "boogie man." She is in real fear of him.

• Her mother is drawn full figured, but without a face. No identity. She is in the background, "waiting on the sidelines." The mother's arms have many lines, and she holds her hands together. This suggests an enormous amount of emotion and sexuality that is held within. In other words, the mother is basically nurturing, but is afraid to express. The mother also has no feet. Her foundation as a woman is missing. She has lost her "footing." She is rendered powerless through her fear of the man. Both Leah and her mother were no doubt subject to the violent outbursts of the father which they felt inadequate to cope with.

• In a situation where there is such a tremendous fear of the father and no real support from the mother, Leah was given little sense of self, little assurance that she was okay as she was. Instead she was learning to be deceptive, to hide truth, to disguise feelings just to get by and "make do" in the situation. There is an underlying terror that if her "real self" is found out, she won't be acceptable. This would carry over in later situations in life whenever she puts someone else in that position of authority. She may go to great efforts to disguise or mask parts of herself until she knows herself and loves herself enough to be open, vulnerable, and real.

• Before she can see the good in her father or men, she must deal with her fear of angry men and her hidden fear that if she lets her anger out, she will be just like her father. She needs to practice dealing with things, as they come up rather than waiting for things to build up and get out of control. It is extremely important that Leah give herself permission to comment on what she sees, what she feels, what she believes, whether it is acknowledged or not. When she knows her own worth, she will have her "footing" as a woman.

Betrayal is the death of trust.

Betrayals happen whenever we feel
used, abandoned, rejected, or sacrificed.
Betrayals are usually the result of unclear
agreements or unrealized expectations.
But no matter how we got hurt, only we
can prolong our pain. We choose how
long we will suffer.

In this chapter, we will learn
how we set ourselves up for betrayal
experiences, what we can learn from
them (don't waste a good betrayal!),
and how we can move beyond pain and
grief to empower ourselves.

Love is expecting people to keep
their agreements
Wisdom is knowing they won't
always do so.
Self-love is loving yourself
even when they don't

CHAPTER 3

Beyond Betrayal

I was six years old when my brother James was born. It was a thrilling event for me. I was no longer the baby in the family! To me he was the most beautiful baby that ever could be. His eyes were bright and laughing. His soft curls fell gently on the nape of his neck. And the smell of Johnson's baby powder that always surrounded him was a sweet incense that intoxicated me.

I became James' "little momma"—his ally and friend. James was a deep and sensitive child who always needed to be comforted in the presence of pain of any kind. I remember once when a bat flew down our chimney. It was thrashing around the living room, knocking things over. In desperation, my mother grabbed a broom and swatted and poked at it, trying to get it out of the house. James immediately burst into tears, afraid the "bird" might get hurt.

The same acute sensitivity was evident in our shared childhood adventures. James would be the one to discover the animal in need and then proceed to become the self-appointed "doctor." And it was James who would insist on conducting proper funerals for any dead animal we discovered on the roads or in the fields.

Aware of his extra antenna, I always felt a need to nurture and protect him, to minimize the disappointments, to soften life somewhat. At Christmas, for example, I would always question my mother ahead of time about what she had bought for James. Then, if I felt the gifts were not appropriate or if she hadn't gotten him enough, I would badger her unmercifully until she bought more.

The empathetic bond continued throughout our growing up years. As we matured, I dropped the care-taking role and our relationship shifted into a more balanced one of mutual support. As adults, James and I both became involved in a spiritual search at the same time. We would frequent the Association of Research and Enlightenment in Virginia Beach, and study the Edgar Cayce readings together. I had first introduced James to the work of Edgar Cayce, and then he, in return, introduced me to Peter and the New Age Center, also at Virginia Beach. As we awakened to the life of the Spirit, we made a trip to Israel together to retrace the paths of early Christianity. Our hours were filled with excited conversation, philosophical discussions, laughter, and precious joy.

But, in time, "it" happened. I was recently divorced and on my own when James approached me about making a fairly substantial loan to him. He wanted to build a house as a speculative venture. At the time, he was investing in an apartment complex he was building, and wanted to borrow as little from the bank as possible for the new house.

We had always been loving and supportive to each other. To me, the matter was simple. I had the money, and he needed it. I loaned him what I had, without any written agreement, signatures, or significant record-keeping. I was content to trust him and collect the monthly interest payments that we agreed upon. The arrangement worked fine—except no buyer for the house or the apartment building appeared.
James' money ran out, the payments stopped—

and James panicked.

Scared and frightened, James made sudden plans to move back to Israel, leaving the unsold house and apartment building behind. Angry and alarmed, I confronted him the night before he left. I accused him. I blamed him. I attacked. Gentle, sensitive James couldn't handle my highly charged emotional state. This was a part of Betty he had never experienced. The nurturing, older sister had suddenly become a "Shrieking War Goddess." Not knowing how to respond, he instinctively reacted with a self-defensive rage.

The next thing I knew he was pushing and shoving me out of his room. In my anger, I turned again toward him, but he fled the room. I followed after James to call him back, but unknown to him, I tripped and sent myself headlong into the wall. I felt my body thud and then I collapsed, unconscious.

When I woke up, there was no one to help me up. I was stunned. Slowly, I got myself together and limped home, trembling, shaken, and confused. I went into the bathroom and began filling the tub with water. It was the only way I knew to nurture myself. I stepped out of my clothes and slipped into the soothing warmth of the water. And then the tears started to flow. I couldn't stop crying. All I had ever known from James was love. How could he do this? Abandon me! Desert me! Hurt me! Anger me! *Betray me!* The hours went by without a word. No phone call, no apology, no heroic commitment to help me out of the specter of debt and insecurity. That day, James left on his desperate exodus to Israel, and I was left with the rubble of broken trust and a life turned upside down.

If this had been my only challenge then, I could have handled it. But this was only the beginning. Within a year, every significant male relationship, every safety net and support system held by the men in my life, would be wrenched away, challenging the woman within me to claim her strength.

As a divorcee, I had already ceased being Mrs. Prominent Attorney's Wife, circulating at country clubs and resting high on the guest list for the best parties. Now, instead of shopping at Bloomingdales, I was struggling to get credit at Sears. And I found myself pitted against my ex-husband in a serious legal battle over real estate holdings.

I was convinced Sean wanted revenge and was taking out his hurt and frustration by using his legal training against me. He had skills, knowledge, and "the system" on his side. We had to deal with each issue, case by case, and the process was long and protracted. One property settlement alone went on for months. After many tense sessions with a mediator, plus three pre-court hearings, the case was settled out of court in my favor. But it was an empty victory. The strain of the constant challenge, accusations, and recriminations had worn me out. Until now, I never had to stand up for myself. Now it seemed that the only thing I was doing was battling and struggling just to survive.

At this same low period, my father died of cancer. He had suffered a long time, and I had watched the disease gradually eat away his body. I felt such empathy for him that I started to develop pre-cancerous conditions myself. Somehow, I had developed a belief I could help my father by taking on his illness. It was a heroic fantasy born from a feeling of powerlessness to help one whom I dearly loved. The belief was irrational, and with some difficulty, I was able to recognize that and let it go. I had to process my own thoughts continuously, weeding out the self-talk of guilt, self-pity, judgement, and criticism and replacing them with supportive ones. The feeling of loss was tremendous when he died. My father loved me unconditionally, and I grew up with a secure feeling that he would always be there when I needed him. Suddenly, there was a void. No open arms. No reassuring voice. Gone were the strength and the wisdom that counseled me. He was dead, and I was unprotected.

About this same time, my fourteen-year-old son John, who was living with me, made a sudden decision to go back and live with his father. He was unhappy with the public school in our new neighborhood, and wanted to return to the private school he had been in before the divorce. So John left me, and my heart sank.

As my financial crisis worsened, I turned to my older brother, John, for help. It took all my courage to pick up the phone. I had to be desperate before I could admit I needed help. I had never done it before. His response was chilling. "I'm sorry, Betty, but my money is all tied up. I can't help you now." John was probably just being honest and clear. But to my vulnerable ears it seemed cold, impersonal. My mind flashed back to warm memories of our happy childhood games and the pride and comfort I had always felt in having him as my brother. But that was then. At this moment I felt a judgement behind his words. I had made a bad decision with James. I had made my own choice to divorce. I would have to live with those results. How different everything seemed now that I was single.

If I had had the courage to confess to John how truly desperate I was, his response would have been different. All my life, he had seen me as confident and capable. In his opinion, my situation might be uncomfortable, but there was nothing to get overly excited about—I could handle it. I was too stuck in my pride to speak out. I was definitely on my own.

My husband, my father, my son, my brothers, all the significant relationships of my past—relationships that had formed my identity, defined who I was, that had given me a sense of security and purpose—were crumbling away, ruptured, and broken by pressures and challenges I had never known before.

It was a painful transition time for me. Yet, it was an exciting time, too. A time of fresh ideas, and new relationships that helped me discover and explore other sides of myself that I had only dimly glimpsed before. There were three people who played big roles during this transitional time. One of them, Francis, was fiery and impulsive with a passion for frank, honest communication, and a commitment to be open. Through him, I began to discover the challenges, the risks, and the beauty of relating in a perfectly honest way, sharing with him all my feelings, thoughts, emotions, fears, and uncertainties. With him, there could be no sham, no games, no masks. I knew through this process, and in this relationship, lay the possibility for uncovering and discovering who I really was. And then, suddenly and without much warning, he moved back to Pennsylvania.

Peter was a spiritual mentor and beloved friend. He, more than anyone else, stirred deep memories in my soul and rekindled an idealism and desire for service that had long been dormant. Peter's wise counsel, humor, and insight helped me through many troubles and blind spots. Peter was the first to really encourage me to teach, giving me the support and validation I needed to begin speaking to groups about dreams, meditation, and personal transformation. When he sensed that I could do this on my own, he pushed me from the nest. As he withdrew, my feeling of loss was as great as the bond I had felt with him was strong.

And then there was Jason. Jason, the imaginative, fun-loving mystic. With Jason, I considered the possibility of a lifelong relationship. But our differences expanded, our philosophies were too divergent and the dream ended.

Throughout this bizarre chain of reversals and unmet expectations, I was being continually thrown back on myself, and myself alone. In countless ways, I felt betrayed. There had been too much loss in too little time.

What Is Betrayal?

Betrayal is the death of trust.

At some time in our lives, most women feel they have been betrayed. Betrayals happen whenever we feel used, abandoned, rejected or sacrificed.

It is important to realize that no other human being is capable of betraying us. The pain may be real, but the betrayal is not. In any situation where we have felt betrayed, someone has simply done what they wanted to do. And we have consented to feel a victim of their action.

A betrayal experience can be as devastating as losing a loved one at death. The same grief and sorrow is there. There seems to be no outlet for the feelings of loss, no source of comfort, no end to the pain.

Our betrayals usually come through someone we love the most—a father who leaves us, a mother who belittles us, a husband who decides that we are no longer exciting, a girlfriend who goes after our man. But there is never a hurt that can't be overcome. And there is never a hurt, beyond the first moment, that is not self-inflicted. Hurts are real, and they can be engendered by other people—but they can only be sustained by us.

The power comes by knowing that no matter what happens to me, I can overcome it. I can turn it around and transform it. Nothing can stop me from being my own fulfilled person. No other person, no matter how they abuse me, can strip me of my rights or rob me of my self-esteem. How I experience myself is my decision.

Love is expecting people to keep their agreements.
Wisdom is knowing that sometimes they won't.
Self-love is knowing you can handle it
when they don't.

How Betrayals Happen

Most betrayals are innocent. We seldom set out to hurt or be hurt by someone. But they do occur. Usually, they are the result of unspoken or unclear agreements. They may also be the result of unrealized or unrealistic expectations.

Innocent Betrayals

When we are children the betrayals come from our parents or other important authority figures, making their impact all the more devastating. And usually the adults involved are quite unaware that the situation is in any way troublesome. The young child feels over-whelmed and is unable to express its deep feelings. The hurt gets buried, often surfacing years later in some dis-guised manner. Or, an expectation that life is going to be full of disappointments begins to build.

Alice, a client, remembered a time when as a young child she had frequent sore throats. The doctors recommended a tonsillectomy. Her parents assured her that having her tonsils out would be quite an adventure. They told her stories about how nice the doctors and nurses would be, how they would take care of her, and even give her a big dish of vanilla ice cream to make her throat feel good.

Alice remembers walking down the sidewalk toward the hospital, firmly holding the hands of both parents and gazing confidently up at the faces of these two people she trusted so completely.

The first evening in the hospital was just as she anticipated: kind doctors and caring nurses taking special care of her, and even the promised ice cream. The next morning, though, was an experience in terror. Excruciating pain woke her. Her throat felt mutilated and raw. Startled and terrified, she tried to call for help, but no words came out. She looked for her parents, but they were gone. There were no doctors or nurses nearby to comfort or explain things to her. Suddenly she felt totally alone and abandoned. Something deep inside died that day. Her throat has long since healed, but Alice is still in pain. Learning to trust is still a big issue in her life.

I think every one of us can remember at least one "innocent betrayal" from our childhood. When I was a little girl, I remember being fascinated with a new box of payons (a very versatile type of paint/crayon) that my sister Joanna had gotten when she began the third grade. The color and the texture of the payons fascinated me, and I asked my mother if I could have a box like Joanna's. "Sure," she replied. "When you get to the third grade, you can have a box, too."

I remembered that promise, and I thought about it often as I imagined and fantasized the drawings and designs I would make. Two years later, when I started the third grade, I asked my mother with great anticipation. "Now can I have my payons?"

My mother had already bought all my school supplies. Her reply was very matter of fact: "You don't need anything else now." I had waited two years, never doubting her promise. I was crushed.

Unspoken Agreements

Betrayals also result from unspoken agreements. Neither party is willing to take responsibility for clarity. The underlying feeling is that if I have to tell him or her what I mean it is just not worth it. Here is a familiar result of not bothering to verbalize an agreement.

Linda is strongly attracted to Ron and decides to become sexually involved. They spend the night together, and in the morning, Linda immediately starts talking about what they will do that evening and how they can spend the upcoming weekend together. Ron starts to feel nervous. "I'm sorry if you've built expectations, but I am not a one-woman man." She feels betrayed.

Unclear Agreements

When we've made an agreement with a close friend, a lover, child, or partner, and these agreements are broken, the deepest wounds are made.

We are most vulnerable in our personal relationships.

Even when we have made what we believe to be clear agreements, we may have a different understanding about what is meant.

In *Annie, Get Your Gun,* a comic operetta popular a few years ago, there was a very humorous but poignant scene that illustrates this point. The hero, a handsome young tenderfoot man from the East, is smitten by Annie, a gun-toting, outspoken, independent woman of the Wild West. Finally he summons up his courage and asks her to marry him, and she joyously agrees. Then in a melodious duet, she sings on one side of the stage of long gowns, fancy parties, and life in the city, while he, on the opposite side, sings of his longings for log cabins, home-spun cloth, and life in the wilds. Betrayal is inevitable.

Unrealized Expectations

When we don't know ourselves, we don't know our

partners. We don't relate to a real person, but to our image of how we want them to be, how we need them to be—and agonize when they don't measure up. The inevitable occurs, breaking our illusions. Always trust people and trust people to be who they are!

Harriet is a divorced woman who feels she needs a man. She begins a relationship with an aspiring lawyer, and all seems to go well. Soon he moves in with her and her two children, and the relationship continues for two years. Her expectation is that he will want the committed relationship and marriage that she wants. Ed is seven years younger than Harriet, and his talk about marriage is vague. After four years, Harriet turns forty, Ed begins talking about how he would really like to have children, and that she is too old. Harriet feels that is an excuse, not the real reason for breaking off the relationship. She senses he doesn't want marriage, period. The relationship ends. She feels betrayed.

Ed is content with compatibility, and there is nothing in his history that indicates that he would commit to marriage and a family. Each of his previous relationships have ended after four or five years. When marriage becomes the ultimate requirement, he bows out. Harriet is in love with the image of who she wants him to be, not who he is.

Moving Beyond Betrayal

One of the best illustrations of how betrayal happens and how to move beyond it is told in the fable, *The Girl with the Silver Hands*. There are many versions of this tale. This is the one I like to tell:

On one of his voyages, a sea captain loses a treasure chest. The Evil One, seeing an opportunity to capture a soul, makes a deal with the captain. He offers to restore the captain's treasure if, in exchange, the Captain will give him the first thing he sees when he walks up the path to his home. The Captain hardly hesitates. In his mind's eye, he sees only the apple tree by the gate. And an apple is a small price to pledge for the return of his treasure. For the rest of the voyage, it's fair wind and full sails. Laden with treasure, the captain forgets his promise.

On his return, as he walks the road to his house, his beautiful daughter—the "apple of his eye"—rushes to him with outstretched arms. She, and not the tree, is the first thing he sees. Through his greed—or limited vision—he has inadvertently betrayed his daughter.

The Captain, with tears in his eyes, and an aching heart, greets his daughter, but keeps his pledge to the devil a secret. That night, she discovers her father's secret. At first she is horrified, and then her horror turns to resignation, and then to anger. To spite the devil and punish her father for his foolish vow, she cuts off her hands and sends them in a box to the Evil One.

The girl runs away from home—fleeing from the father and all that he represents—and is guided by angels to a beautiful garden, where she lives. Without hands, she has no way to feed herself. But the angels stay by her, whispering that she must stand on her toes to eat the berries and fruits that hang abundantly above her head.

Our heroine lives in her garden undisturbed until one day a King discovers the garden and falls in love with her. His royal silversmiths fashion beautiful hands for her. Soon she becomes pregnant, but before she can tell him the news, he leaves her to go fight a war in a foreign country.

Meanwhile, the Evil One is enraged at being cheated out of his prize. With the king gone, the Evil One enters into an alliance with the Queen Mother and, *through the agency of vicious rumors which she starts to spread, manages to turn the kingdom against the girl with the silver hands. This time she is forced to flee, and in the wilderness, she gives birth to her child, whom she names Sorrowful.*

Weak with thirst, she discovers an abandoned well—a deep source of spiritual nourishment and life. A mysterious and powerful voice speaks deep from within the well, telling her to put her hands in the water. She protests.

"I have no hands," she says.

Again the voice urges, "Put your hands in the water."

This time she does—and the magic happens. She feels a tremendous release from her sorrow and pain, and when she withdraws her hands from the water, she discovers they are whole and real again.

Symbolically, her hands represent her power. When she severs her hands, she cuts herself off from her own power, and gives it over to the dark force, the hidden or unconscious part of the self. Consciously or unconsciously, many women cut themselves off from their own power after a betrayal.

Even when we give away our power, in our deepest hurts and wounds, there is a way to feed and nourish ourselves—if we will listen to our guidance. In fairy tales, myths, and folklore, supernatural beings, like angels and animals—creatures from nature—provide answers and show the way out of impossible situations. They represent guidance from the higher parts of ourselves.

The woman who willfully cuts off her hands in reaction to the unintentional, but thoughtless action of her father, regains her strength by following the voice that comes from a deep, nourishing—but abandoned—

place. By dipping her wounds into the very source of life, the depths of her spirit, all that she lost is restored to her.

This story affirms for women that no matter how horrendous the experience has been, no matter how much trauma, sadness, or grief there has been, there is a time when it must end. And the end will come when we, like the girl with the silver hands, are willing to put our hands in the water. Putting our hands in the water is another way of saying we must get in touch with our own deep feelings and move through them. We need to accept the sorrow, release the rage, shed the tears, and then reclaim our power. And we must do it alone. Though we can be helped along the way, no one ultimately can do it for us.

The sorrow ends and living begins when we begin to trust that deep inner voice that speaks from our own depths, and urges us to move on with our lives.

That year when I experienced so many betrayals was one of pure tragedy. My feelings of self-worth and self-love were low at that time, and I created a drama, scene by scene, where I invited every significant male in my life to dismiss me—to put me out of their lives in one way or another.

But on another level, the drama that I created served a much greater purpose. All my life I had lots of males to support me, to care for, acknowledge, and encourage me. Because of that, the greater part of my "maleness," my inner strength, lay dormant. Through the dramatic series of events, I was invoking some powerful challenges—"mythic tasks"—that would empower my male side and would focus my strength and vision more clearly. With no wise or strong man around to supply answers or security, I was forced to go within to the Source of my own being and totally listen and trust my own inner guidance.

We create the world we live in, giving people very

specific communications about how they are to treat us. If we have low self-esteem, for example, we will give out that communication, and people will respond on cue to the roles we have chosen to play. When we can change ourselves, we automatically will change the way we allow others to treat us.

When I could love myself and claim my "maleness"—instead of projecting it on others and giving it away—I rewrote the script, and all my relationships began to re-form. Instead of tragic melodrama, I began creating an adventure, with romance, humor, joy, and personal fulfillment.

Yes, we need to grieve for the enormous losses we feel. And then we need to start living again. I learned a very valuable lesson about betrayal. It is hard to let go of the pain and resentments. But it is a lot harder and more painful not to.

Sharing The Gold Of My Betrayal

One of the most humbling things about writing this book was to learn that "I" was not writing it. From the beginning, it seemed as if the book had a life of its own, and that a Higher Force, a Consciousness different from my own, was directing it. Throughout the entire writing process, undeniable situations, synchronicities of events, people, situations appeared almost on cue with each chapter that continually forced me to deal with the very thing I was writing about in a personal and confrontive way. It was almost as if something was saying. "You are not going to write about theories or other people's experiences—every lesson is yours!"

While organizing the "Betrayal" chapter, I was closeted off in a small room in the foothills of the Blue Ridge Mountains of Virginia. During that time alone, I was able to confront the hurts that I had been carrying within for several years, but had so conveniently stuffed. Those periods when we are able to interface with ourselves are very significant—and can't be forced. When the time is ripe, the memories and feelings bubble up into the conscious realm quite naturally.

During those three days alone, my tears could not stop flowing. It was as though I had started to unravel an endless cord with knots, one knot connected to another, each one with unexpressed feelings and unfinished business. One by one I pulled them out, my memories so interconnected with each other that it was difficult to know where one began and another ended. And when the sadness or the feeling of loss become too overwhelming, I would take warm baths, once at four in the morning. The warm enfolding of the water was a source of calm and solace, like resting in the bosom or womb of the Great Mother.

One thing was clear. It was up to me to heal the pain of my betrayals. The one with the most sting was the one with James, my brother. I had lived with that pain for three years, hanging on to my belief that I was right about how he had wronged me.

On the third night, I was awakened abruptly, with these words running through my mind, "No one else can betray you. You can only betray yourself." It was as if some deep realization had been gestating deep within my own unconscious, and now, in this room, it was given birth. It was a truth that went beyond any intellectualism, or philosophical concept. It was a deep, penetrating, uncompromising experience with what is Real. The only betrayal that is real is when we betray ourselves by allowing some person or situation to separate us from our real nature—which is Love!

By remaining righteously indignant and rationalizing my position, I had cut myself off from James. I needed to stop looking at what James did to me and look instead at what I was doing to myself. Instead of being immobilized in the hurt and pain of the past, I began to search instead for the beliefs, the program-ming, the conditioning, and patterns of the past that were operating on an unconscious level and had attracted such an experience.

When James approached me about borrowing the money, I wanted to keep "everything nice." I avoided taking a stand, and, out of fear of confrontation, was not direct in my communication with him. As a result, our agreements were not clear. I had gone into an emotional fog, naively hoping that everything would work out all right. But underneath the Pleasing Passive exterior was an imbedded, underlying terror of being responsible for myself. My unvoiced fear was that I couldn't handle my situation alone, and I maintained a false value about money as my security.

To realize something is one thing, to put it into practice is another. In order to own it, I needed to do something about it. And so, that morning I wrote a letter to James. I acknowledged my part in our three-year scenario. I also told him the truth: I was hurting. I loved him and our separation was painful. Holding back love always is. I wanted to drop the whole incident and no longer hold him responsible or accountable for the past.

The last time I had seen James was on Thanks-giving Day and we had sat awkwardly at separate tables and had exchanged only a few polite comments. This time when James saw me it was at another family func-tion. His eyes twinkled, and he grinned and hugged me warmly. That one moment was worth everything. The past was past. We were loving again, and I had come home to my true self.

A friend of mine shared with me a catharsis she experienced at the Wailing Wall in Jerusalem. The tradition is for the pilgrim to write a prayer on a piece of paper and place it in a crack in the wall. Rachel's prayer was for the release of her grief. As she placed it between two ancient bricks, she was suddenly overwhelmed with emotion, and cried out, "I don't want to wail anymore." Tears began to flow, and the burden and pain from forty years of blaming loved ones for her disappointments and despair was lifted from her.

Like Rachel, many women are seduced by the bittersweet melancholy of acting out the role of the "wronged woman."

Sadness is seductive, and the more intense and deeper the suffering, the more the enmeshment. Like the girl with the silver hands, or Rachel at the Wailing Wall, we must face our sorrow. Once we acknowledge both the part we played in the experience and what we learned from the experience, we can emerge healed and whole.

The Flying Boy

Helen recognized her pattern with men followed her father's example. He was a Peter Pan, the little boy that never grew up—a "flying boy" as the poet Robert Blye describes them. Her father was never there when she needed him. Flighty and irresponsible, this type of man is in constant need of a mother. He is out of touch with his own maleness and incapable of commit-ment and long-term relationships.

Over and over again, Helen had felt betrayed by men. But all the men she chose were just like her father.

A year later she wrote to tell me that she knew she was through with that pattern. For the first time in her life, she was in a relationship with a supportive male who was settled and established in his profession. She had forgiven her father and accepted her responsibility for creating a mature relationship.

Daddy's Little Princess

Sarah tearfully shared how, as a little girl, she had always been Daddy's little princess. As she became older, he seemed to suddenly turn on her. Instead of the warm praise and constant attention she was accustomed to, she was accused of being sexually promiscuous—even before she knew the meaning of the term! She couldn't understand his change of heart—and she felt outraged and betrayed by his name-calling and innuendos.

Sarah's realization was that her father had been drawn to her sexually in her adolescence. His sexual urges toward his pubescent daughter confused him, and he repressed those feelings and projected his guilt on her. Sarah understood that her father's emotional confusion had nothing to do with her worth as a woman. Once her own confusion cleared, she could gain back her own self-esteem, and, with deep compassion and understanding, forgive her father.

Cold-Hearted Father

In Amsterdam, Annika, a young Dutch girl, confronted a deep resentment toward her father. She described her father as an intellectual who spent most of his time in his study and who was devoid of love or joy. He had neither been affectionate nor emotionally supportive.

But what jolted Annika was the realization that she had developed a pattern similar to his. By blaming her father for his emotional deprivation, she cut herself off from her own power to create the joy and love she needed so badly to give to herself and to others.

If our loved ones don't or can't give us what we

need, then we must give it to ourselves. It doesn't help to blame someone for not doing something they aren't able or capable of doing. Annika's father gave her all the love that he was capable of giving at that time. It was the best he understood. The fact that it wasn't enough or sufficient for her needs doesn't matter now. What matters is that Annika needed to realize how much pain she had perpetrated on herself by demanding her father be different than he actually was, and that she could now forgive him and get on with her life.

Experiential Exercises
For Moving Beyond Betrayal

Exercise One: A Letter To My Self

(to be done alone)

In the very center of each of us there is a source of life, a core self which knows exactly what we need at any given moment. The single most important thing we can do in life is to get in touch with this core self.

The following exercise is designed to help communicate with your core self. This can be a very useful tool to deal with the deep pain of betrayal.

It is best to allow a whole evening for this exercise. Take the phone off the hook and protect yourself from interruptions as best as you can. Make your space private and sacred.

All you need is a pen and paper. You are going to write a letter to your inner self. Begin the letter, "Dear Inner Self" or "Dear Teacher," or use whatever name invokes trust, love, empathy, compassion, wisdom, or understanding for you. (Spirit, Soul, Christ, Master, *etc*).

Assume that your inner teacher loves you more than you love yourself and has no need to judge or criticize you for whatever you have done, no matter what it is. You are free to express any and all feelings.

Take time to get in touch with the experience that carries the most pain for you. You may need to look at old photographs to evoke feelings and memories, or to play favorite music to carry you into the experience.

When you feel ready, begin to write freely and honestly about all your feelings surrounding that experience and time. Whatever was not said, say it now. Spend as long as it takes to get out all the emotions and beliefs. And know that your inner self knows, accepts, and understands.

When you have completed your letter, ask yourself if you are ready to move beyond the pain. If you are, decide that this experience no longer has power over you and affirm that you are free of its impact or ability to influence your life.

Now look for the gold in that betrayal. What can you gain from it? Follow the steps outlined on page 115.

First, identify the value. Be sure you know what it is. Write it down to fix it in your mind.

Next, claim your gold powerfully!

Then, decide how you are going to Follow Through, and act on it!

Exercise Two: Sharing and Listening

(To be done with a partner)

In this exercise, two friends agree to support each other in moving beyond betrayal. Arrange conditions which will insure uninterrupted time for this special sharing. Sit across from each other (cross legged on the floor works well) with a lighted candle beside you.

One friend begins by talking freely about a time in which she felt betrayed. She may have to talk briefly about several incidents until she uncovers one with a lot of impact. The partner is there to love this person, supporting her enough that she feels safe in opening up to her hurts, her pain, and her inner self.

The partner listens only. This is not a time to give opinions or make judgments or even to sympathize. If you are listening and your partner gets stuck, you may ask a leading question to help move her to clarity. For example, "How did you feel when that happened?" Or, "What was that experience like for you, when he said . . . ?"

When the speaker has finished her story, the next step is to dismiss that experience from having any more power in her life.

Then dig for gold. The speaker identifies and affirms what she has gained from the betrayal. Again, the partner is there to listen, and to help support the speaker in uncovering new depth and power from the betrayal by asking questions, if possible. "What beliefs do you want to change or let go of? What value has it had for you? How has the experience made you stronger, more sensitive, *etc.*?"

The two partners switch roles, and begin the process again. This time the first speaker is the listener, and the listener shares her story.

When both partners have completed the process, they take the candle in their hands (symbolizing the Light of Truth) and, holding it up together, lift it above their heads while facing each other. Each partner takes turns forgiving and releasing the persons and the experience. Next, each states boldly the gold they have received from the betrayal and affirms their responsibility for creating their own joy!

When the shared light of understanding is held high, it is a powerful moment!

Love is expecting people to keep their
    agreements.
Wisdom is knowing that sometimes
    they won't.
Self-love is knowing you can handle it
    when they don't.

Guidelines For Moving Beyond Betrayal

1. Acknowledge Your Feelings

Talk out your feelings and emotions with an attentive, receptive partner. Until a person feels that he or she has been really listened to, there can be no resolution. If there is no supportive partner available, write your feelings out in a journal.

2. Change Your Perspective

Understand the others involved in the situation. What were they thinking and feeling? What were their fears, expectations, assumptions? How did they experience the situation? Release and forgive!

Your own belief systems helped create this situation. The other person was only an agent acting out your own reality.

3. Claim The Value

The value is always there when we can understand our betrayal experience—not for the pain it produces but for the opportunity for healing and growth that it offers. Don't waste a good betrayal! Get the "gold" from it.

The following is a partial list of values you may have gained from the betrayal experience:

Identify the belief, conditioning, programming that is no longer working for you. (Make a decision to blast through it!)

Are you stronger, more compassionate, clearer about what you want or don't want in your life?

Break through projections and illusions about a person and love and accept them as they are (not as you want them to be).

Decide to ask for what you want.

Decide to speak up sooner in the future.

Decide to own your power, rather than giving it away.

Decide to create supportive relationships in your life.

Decide to be true to your own beliefs.

Decide to develop a stronger spiritual focus in your life.

4. Follow Through

Take positive steps to put your new understanding into practice. It requires a new response to an old practice. You may need to phone, write, or get with the person or persons that you felt betrayed by in order to complete the process. Follow through also includes making steps in a positive direction in your life (join a support group, change your environment into a supportive atmosphere, *etc.*)

Visualization is a must in healing relationships and for changing negative patterns. Each day relax for a few minutes, close your eyes and focus on the person who betrayed you, seeing them in a positive way (happy, smiling, laughing, singing, confident). Now see yourself at peace with that person.

You may have to repeat this exercise many times before you get results. But it works. Keep practicing! Continue as long as needed.

* * *

You know you have moved beyond
betrayal when what you have learned from
the experience equals or surpasses the
amount of pain that you have invested in it.

* * *

The ability to transform life's experiences is not new. It has been known in many ancient cultures, including the Native American. They have a respect and understanding of the power of the four elements. As women, we too can tap into the transformational energy of these elements.

CHAPTER 4

Practicing Your Magic

The Sweat Lodge Ceremony And The Power Of The Four Directions

A few years ago in Virginia Beach, I was invited to participate in a Native American Sweat Lodge ceremony. I had no idea what a sweat lodge was, except that it was a traditional purification ceremony of the American Indian. I had great respect for the Native American's reverence for nature, and was curious about their spiritual traditions, so I decided to experiment.

The ceremony began with a group of men and women sitting around a roaring fire. The shaman stood in the center, close to the fire, and began the ceremony by drawing deeply on his long-stemmed pipe, and making an offering of smoke to each of the "grandfathers," the guardian spirits of the four directions. Then the group entered the sweat lodge, crawling on our hands and knees through the small opening in front of the fire. The lodge was a low dome built from bent saplings covered with black plastic and insulated by blankets and sleeping bags to hold in the heat. Inside, the lodge was pitch black with only space enough to squat.

"This is the womb of Mother Earth," the shaman

said, "which we enter in order to be reborn."

There was some nervous laughter and giggling as we entered and jostled and jiggled and squirmed in the darkness, squatting elbow to shoulder until we were all settled into place. The shaman was the last to enter and signaled for the first of the rocks to be brought in.

Seven rocks, heated to a red-hot intensity, were taken from the fire and placed in the pit in the center of the lodge. The flap was lowered, plunging us into total darkness, except for the white glow of the rocks.

The sharp pungent odor of sage and cedar filled the lodge as the shaman threw sacred herbs on the rocks, followed by sputtering and sizzling as he began ladling water over the rocks. My eyes began to water from the smoke, and my skin felt seared by the sudden rise in temperature from the steam.

No one spoke, and the shaman began offering prayers to the "grandfathers," invoking their presence in the lodge. My reactions were mixed. "Do I really have to sweat and bake to become spiritual?" I thought. I was dubious and resistant, and I felt curious rather than expectant.

"Are these people really into this?" I wondered with a feeling of ridicule, "Or are they just kidding?" Virginia Beach is fertile soil for every new thing!

As the others began to pray, some called upon the grandfathers, using Native American images that seemed strange and unnatural to me. Others prayed in more traditional language, calling upon God, Jesus, or the Holy Spirit. Some of the prayers seemed interminable. As the heat increased, so did my discomfort and my cynicism.

"What have I gotten myself into! How long is this going to go on! I am definitely not an Indian!" I thought. Finally, the shaman ordered the flap to be opened, indicating the first round was over, and asked for more rocks to be brought in.

"God forbid, the rocks should get cool!" someone muttered next to me. The flap was lowered, and the heat and sound of the sizzling steam filled the crowded, dark space.

"If you think it gets too hot in here," the shaman said, "look at that belief—and move beyond it. If you think it is too crowded in here—look at that limitation and move beyond it. Look at all your beliefs, and let them go. Become one with the power in the rocks. Call upon the grandfathers!"

The sweat was dripping off my body. The heat and discomfort was breaking down my ego structure. My will, my defenses were being weakened, dismantled by the heat and intensity of the ceremony.

"Look at your mind—watch how it works. Your ego creates limitations. Let it die. Be strong, like the earth. Feel the fire, let it free you."

Time was suspended. I had no idea how long I had been in the sweat lodge—or indeed, if it would ever end. My cynicism, my ridicule melted in the heat and I kept moving deeper into the experience, deeper into myself. The sweat lodge was concentrating and accelerating a spectrum of feelings, emotions, and memories. It was uncomfortable and seemed endless. But I was no longer concerned with my reactions, or with the people around me. There were sighs and low groans. Someone was crying. But the heat was no longer an obstacle. I gave up fighting and began moving with it. The shaman shook his rattle and began chanting.

The rocks glowed dimly in the center of the lodge. My attention was drawn to them. The center of the circle. It was a place of power, of wholeness, where earth, fire, water, air had become transformed into one powerful force that was moving me into the light, into a new place of vision within myself. There was no sense of separation. Separation comes from resistance. And without resistance, there is only oneness.

Finally, the flap opened for the last time, letting in a hint of the cool night air from the outside. Never had I sensed a soothing breeze with such heartfelt appreciation, or so acutely.

I struggled out from the lodge, and was enveloped by the night air. My body drank in its presence, and I rejoiced in a sacred moment. I walked to a pine tree and stretched out on the ground beneath it and looked up through its branches at the moon and stars. All the toxins in my body seemed to be drawn out, absorbed by the earth beneath me. Again, the simple act of lying on the ground felt very sacred, as if the strong, silent power of "Mother Earth," was protecting, enfolding, nurturing me.

The words of the shaman were true. In the lodge we return to the womb of Mother Earth to be reborn to all parts of ourselves:

To the earth that is our strength
To the water that is our life.
To the air that is formless and free.
To the fire that purifies and consumes.

Invoking The Power
Of The Four Elements

In the ancient cultures, one of the marks of a true magician was his or her ability to control the elements. The magician/priest or priestess was not simply an illusionist or trickster, but rather a master of subtle energies and life-force who was in control of, and not controlled by, situations, circumstances, or external events.

In the following sections, we will explore ways of

getting in touch with other dimensions of our inner self that are felt or sensed, but not easily articulated. The qualities that we will be invoking are symbolized by the four elements—Earth, Water, Air, and Fire. Each element represents a differentiated power or archetypal energy that is available to us and can be called upon to aid us in awakening, activating, and expressing latent qualities or dimensions of our wholeness that have been dormant, or of which we are not fully conscious.

In a previous chapter, we learned to "own" the Bitch and call her by name in order to dismiss her false power. Whenever we dismiss a negative energy, we must replace it with something positive; otherwise the Bitch will return.

This is where our magic begins. We get to choose earth, air, fire, or water. By learning the names—and the essence—of these elements, we can empower that energy within us. They are four aspects of true power!

Element Earth

The energy within us that is
PRACTICAL, FOCUSED, RATIONAL, GROUNDED,
LEFT-BRAIN, LINEAR, LOGICAL, CLEAR, DETAILED

"Lord, teach me to accept the things that can't be changed, change those things that can be changed, and the wisdom to know the difference."

In this famous prayer, St. Francis echoes the spirit of the "earth" element. It is not a prayer of resignation, but an invocation for clarity. The element of earth gives us the ability to see through appearances, masks, and roles to the heart or essence of what is.

In certain Native American traditions, the spirit of the earth resides with the grandfather of the West. That "grandfather" bestows upon his children the strength to give expression or form to their true spiritual nature and purpose. In esoteric Judeo-Christian traditions, the spirit of the earth element is represented by the archangel Uriel.

A Persian Folktale

The spirit of the "earth" is reflected beautifully in this simple Persian folktale.

There once was a farmer. He was very poor; and then his father died and left him several beautiful horses—stallions and mares.

The next day, when his wife went to the village, the people said to her. "Oh, how lucky you are now that your husband owns several beautiful stallions."

"I don't know if I am lucky or not," said she. "All I know is that my husband now owns several beautiful horses, both stallions and mares."

That night, the horses broke through the farmer's little corral and ran off into the hills with a herd of wild horses.

"Oh, what bad luck," the people of the village said the next morning as they crowded around the empty corral. "Just as we feared, thieves have come and stolen your beautiful horses."

"Is it good luck or bad? You decide," the woman replied. "I only know the horses are gone."

A few days later, the wife awoke to find the horses back in the corral. Not only had the horses returned, but the herd had increased. A dozen wild horses had followed them home. When the people of the village heard the news, they came out to the farm to congratulate the farmer and his wife on their good fortune.

"Oh, how lucky you are," they said. "You have more horses now than you did before." And the woman

answered, *"I don't know if it is lucky or not. All I know is that we now have more horses."*

When it came time to break the horses, the farmer's son, who was a bold and dashing young man, chose the most magnificent and powerful of the wild stallions as his own. When he tried to break it, the stallion threw him to the ground and trampled on his leg. His leg was injured so severely that he was permanently crippled.

"Oh, curse your bad luck," the people said.

"My son is crippled. But who can say if it's bad luck or not," the woman answered as she went her way.

A short while later, the Caliph declared war on a neighboring kingdom. All the young men in the country were conscripted for military duty, but the farmer's son was exempt because of his leg.

When all the sons and husbands had gone off to fight, the women of the town commended her on her good fortune.

"You are very lucky," they said. "Your son doesn't have to go to war."

And she replied, "All I know is that my son doesn't have to go to war."

In this story, the farmer's wife looks at things as they are—without interpretation or embellishment, without fantasizing about fears of the future. She accepts what happens amid the changing circumstances and vacillating opinions of others. She remains centered.

She is as solid and grounded as the earth she walks upon.

Like the farmer's wife, we can call upon the "earth element" whenever we need to become solid and stable.

If the earth element is missing, we won't deal directly, openly, or honestly with issues. For example, has there ever been a time when you walked into a room, and an associate—a friend or lover—didn't speak to you? What assumptions did you make about why they didn't speak?

How did you interpret the look on their face?

What came up for you?

Our minds work at terrific speeds, and the amount of internal dialogue that gets triggered by the smallest nuances of behavior, the tiniest inflection or facial movement, is staggering.

Are they mad at me?

Are they avoiding me?

What did I do wrong?

The truth of the situation is that you entered the room and someone didn't speak to you. Perhaps the reason they didn't notice you is because they didn't have their contacts in. It can be that simple.

Getting Grounded

Too often, as women, we get pulled in so many directions. At one time, our highest priority may be taking care of a baby. At another time, the most important focus might be starting a business, beginning a career—or getting our health in order! Which is more valuable? Which is more important? In our career-driven and result-oriented society, the self image of many of us is caught up on a false sense or belief that "I am what I do." Which of those roles are who we really are?

There is a myth about the goddess Psyche, in which she is given four very difficult tasks. One of the four challenges Psyche faces in the process of becoming a goddess is to sort and separate an enormous pile of seeds. She is overwhelmed by the task and collapses in despair. An army of ants appears and does the sorting for her.

One of the tasks of every woman is to straighten

her priorities. She needs to learn how to separate and sort out the many claims that are made on her time and energy. The ants which rescued Psyche from her insoluble dilemma represent that part of us that is orderly and structured. We need to call upon it and claim it to help us become clear, and not be pulled in every direction by feelings or emotions and the pull of others. In times when we are feeling confused, uncertain, powerless, or overwhelmed, if we can get still and quiet long enough to get the despairing self out of the way, that natural and orderly part of ourselves will come forward to do the "sorting and sifting."

Keeping focused, keeping priorities straight, and being practical and grounded are all qualities we need at appropriate times. By invoking the spirit of the earth within us, we can claim the power to keep our feet on the ground and our minds clear.

A Story Of Earth

EVERYTHING IS JUST FINE

Grace was a meticulous, well-groomed, fifty-year-old woman who was obsessive with her fastidiousness. With Grace, there was never a hair out of place; everything was perfect. Except that a third of her stomach had just been removed, her energy was low, her relationship with her husband was strained, and she was having a very difficult time adjusting to the chemotherapy.

Grace was a cancer patient. She was recovering from surgery when she came for counseling. In the first two sessions with her, no real progress was made. Invariably her response was, "Everything is just fine." In our third session, I experienced an unmistakable intuitive flash. Suddenly I had an impression of a woman and a name.

"Grace, who is Eve?" I asked, puzzled by the image.

Grace winced slightly as if she had been struck, and her eyes filled with tears. Awkwardly at first, and then effortlessly, she poured out a story which she had kept hidden for years. Eve had been the "other woman."

"I knew about her for years," Grace confessed. "She worked in my husband's company. At first I refused to believe he was having an affair, and then I couldn't ignore it—the weekends out of town, the hushed phone calls, the glances between them. But I never could bring myself to say anything to him about it."

Grace had kept the hard, bitter resentment inside her. She literally couldn't "stomach" the betrayal, and her pain and grief had been eating away inside her all this time. In all those many years, this was the first time she openly acknowledged her real hurt. Everything wasn't fine. It hadn't been for a long time. She was now ready to honestly look at what really *is*, rather than pretending. The healing process could begin.

Earth gives us the ability to see what is and to name it clearly. Earth is the strength to be honest and to accept the truth that sets us free. In other words, don't let doubts, fears, depressions, or emotional confusion rob you of your focus and clarity. Keep centered, keep moving.

Don't let anything take your strength away.

Call upon the earth.

Invoking The Earth

AN EXERCISE FOR GAINING CLARITY

Many women simply want to be unhappy, and so they play a game called "I don't have what I need to have in order to be happy," and this allows them to indulge their Bitch by feeling miserable and discontent, and blaming something or someone for the way they feel. I often use a process for helping women become clear on what it is that they want.

The focus of the process is quite simple. We begin by asking the person what it is they think they want, and then we ask, "If you could have it right now, would you take it?" Invariably, body language, tone of voice, facial expressions, eye contact (or lack of it), and other indicators show if the person is really clear about what they want, or if it is camouflage for the Bitch. If there is ambiguity and uncertainty, we work until we get clear on what it is they really want.

For example, Betty wanted to be a therapist. She had been accepted to graduate school and had recently begun her studies. When asked what she wanted, she replied without hesitation, "I want to complete my studies and begin my practice." She looked directly at the group as she spoke. She communicated determination and unswerving self-confidence. And the group had no trouble agreeing unanimously that she would get what she wanted.

Terri stood up next and declared that she wanted a relationship. During the workshop, Terri had complained because there wasn't a significant male in her life. When she declared to the group, her voice was weak, her words lacked authority, and she looked slightly to the side. Terri was unclear. Through the process of restructuring her declaration, Terri finally realized that what she really wanted was not a relationship with its conditions and restrictions, but a male friend in her life.

When she got clear about that, she could let go of her anger and resentment about not being in a relationship. She didn't want one in the first place. Sometimes, in order to cut through the emotional fog and confusion, we need to call upon the clear, powerful, grounding energy of the earth.

The following exercise is a simple five-step process for invoking that element.

A FIVE-STEP PROCESS FOR GAINING CLARITY

(This can be done with a partner, support group, or by yourself in front of a mirror. When doing it by yourself, stare in the mirror and watch your own facial reactions carefully).

1. State what it is you think you want.

This can be anything that you feel is important or heartfelt: a goal you want to achieve, a quality you want to develop, an experience you wish to have, something you want to cause to happen, to create or to establish (a vacation plan, career change, relationship, *etc.*).

2. Notice what you are communicating.

Do your body language, tone of voice, choice of words, facial expression, *etc.*, support your communication, or does anything indicate confusion, lack of clarity, or signal a mixed message. Ask your partner or group to report what they observe.

3. Repeat your declaration until everyone present agrees it is confident and clear.

4. If I had it now, would I take it?

Have your partner or someone in the group ask you that question. Be as clear as you can about the implications of getting what you want. Is it what you *really* want? For example, if getting what you want means leaving the area where you live, or restructuring your life-style in a significant way—would you still want it? What are your priorities?

If you can't answer the question with an unqualified "yes," restructure your statement, refining it as often as you need to, until you can. For example, Terri started out stating she wanted a relationship. But she lacked confidence and authority affirming it. It was obvious she was ambivalent about what she thought she wanted. And if you send out confusion, you get back confusion. It took several attempts before she came up with a statement she really supported. When Terri said, "I want a male friend," she was clear.

5. When you have come to clarity, notice how you feel and share it with those present (or write it in your journal).

Learn to do this process in your own thoughts when you need to invoke the "earth" element within you. Say to yourself, "I invoke the power and clarity of the earth," and visualize yourself standing firmly on the fertile soil of Mother Earth.

Element Water

The energy within us that is
INTUITIVE, FLEXIBLE, NURTURING, FEELING, YIELDING, VULNERABLE, RECEPTIVE

"Are you Michael?"

I held up my nameless, newborn son in my arms and balanced him on my chest, and listened for a response, a confirmation.

"Are you. . .Aaron?" I asked again and waited for a stirring, a recognition, a feeling, a bond. And again, nothing. My husband and I had pored over baby books with hundreds of names. We had narrowed the list down to a dozen. Now, none seemed to fit. "Are you Scott? Brook?" I repeated this little ritual several times over the next day, each time with a different name. I knew there was a right name, the name this soul wanted, and I knew he would tell me—but I didn't know how. And on the third day, I asked:

"Well, are you John?" Suddenly a rush of energy surged from the crown of my head and swept through my body down to my toes. It was an incredible moment. "Yes, your name is John."

In the medicine wheel, the North is the direction that points to creative darkness that is the womb of winter. Winter is the season where all life grows still and quiet. It is a time of incubation. And out of that void, all life proceeds. To the Grandfather of the North is entrusted the secrets and the mystery that is the source of life itself. This is the element of water.

Water is the element that gives a woman power to be still, to be receptive, reflective, and intuitive. The most "feminine" of the elements in its gentleness and its strength, water represents the power of nurturing, caring, feeling, and all the qualities most fully present in women.

Receptivity is not to be confused with passivity. The receptive woman who is in touch with the spirit of "water" senses her own value and worth. Her decisions and responses are quite conscious and come from a place of knowingness within her. On the other hand, the passive woman gives her power away by not being honest with her feelings or responding openly to the situations or people around her.

Perhaps the most important characteristic of "water" is the ability to listen, and to be open. Openness is born of a desire to understand. To truly understand ourselves and others, we must listen not with the head and ears alone, but with the heart. To hear with the heart takes skill, patience, and a willingness to be open, vulnerable, and flexible.

Centuries ago, this skill was regarded much more

seriously than now. For example, the Greek philosopher, Pythagoras, was one of the most brilliant philosophers of the Classical Age. In the school he established, students who were accepted for training were first taken to a statue of a veiled Muse. The statue showed the Muse with her finger raised to her lips, indicating silence. In front of this great statue, the students took a vow of silence which lasted from two to five years. This discipline forced them to develop the highly-prized gifts of receptivity and intuition.

The Light Of A Holy Presence Here

Some of the most challenging experiences that I have had in learning to follow the flow of the intuitive "water" energy and to trust my heart have been in working with patients. Esther was a critically ill heart patient. I had been counseling her for some time. She was a delightful, spunky personality, and our sessions together had always been meaningful. One night, long after normal visiting hours, I felt a strong urge to stop by the hospital to see her. I was finished for the day, and I wasn't scheduled to see Esther again for another few days.

When I entered the room, I knew immediately my intuition to see her was correct. The room was dark, and Esther was seated on the edge of the bed, terrified. I sensed that her death was near—and that she knew it.

"I had a dream last night," she said morosely. "I dreamed I was in a long, dark tunnel. It was frightening. I never felt so alone and scared in my life. I kept moving, going through the tunnel. But I never got to the end. And then I woke up, and I haven't been able to shake this feeling all day."

Esther looked up at me and smiled forlornly, and I reached out to hold her hand. The dream reflected her own fear and unresolved feelings about death. The emotions were so strong that she couldn't experience the dream all the way through. There was no light for her at the end of the tunnel.

And again, I had to listen, and trust my intuition.

"Esther," I said, "I think it's important that you go back into your dream and bring it to completion."

She was frightened at the suggestion, but she trusted me enough to lead her through a guided reverie as we re-experienced the dream. I held her hand, and we recited her favorite psalm together. . . "He who dwells in the secret place of the most High shall say of the Lord, you are my God. In Him do I trust. . . . "

As we prayed together, Esther entered the tunnel again, and this time, in the distance, she saw a golden orb of light and began moving toward it. At the end of the tunnel, she found her husband, who had died several years earlier, waiting for her.

"There is a sense of a Holy Presence here," she said, "And now he has me by the hand, and we're walking into the Light, and, and. . . it's so beautiful." She stopped and tears flooded her eyes. Suddenly, she saw her mother and father and other loved ones coming toward them out of the Light. The sense of a Holy Presence grew stronger, replacing her fears with peace.

When I left her, she was peaceful and unafraid, and there was a delicate, pure glow surrounding her. Shortly after I arrived at home that night, the phone rang. It was the hospital. Esther had passed away.

It was a very powerful experience for me. And I was thankful that I trusted what I knew. A very wise and important teacher, Edgar Cayce, once said that the more intuitively based our decisions are, the deeper and more far-reaching the results will be. Listening for inner guidance and then acting upon it is the only way to develop intuition. The more we listen, the more we'll

hear. But it doesn't grow, until we act upon what
we know.

The Second Son Is Doubt

The wisdom and spiritual insight of the *I Ching*,
or *Book of Changes,* has guided and nurtured the soul
of China for over three thousand years. In the *I Ching*,
a story is told to explain how intuition works.

In the beginning, there was Heaven and Earth. The
first born of their union was a child named "Intuition."
On the heels of this first son came a second,
named "Doubt."

Heaven is a symbol of consciousness or soul, and
Earth a symbol for the body, or the physical self. From
the union, or harmony, or interplay between these two,
our intuitive feelings are born. But invariably, our logical,
rational mind takes over and begins to question, doubt,
or second-guess that inner knowing.

"Oh, that can't be right—it doesn't make
any sense!"

"It's only my imagination!"

"It's just a fantasy."

"I'd better think that one through again."

These are all the voices of doubt, born on the heels
of intuitive insight. And at times like these, the *I Ching*
advises, "Go to the High Mountain." When doubt is born,
return to the stillness—to receptivity—and there you will
find your "first born" again.

There is a story about one of the great Chinese
masters. It is said that one day while meditating in his
room, he heard a noise in the courtyard. When he
looked out the window, he saw a stork and a snake fighting. Every time the snake thrust forward, the bird would
yield, and brush the snake aside with its wing. He observed that the struggle was like a dance, a merging of

active and passive energies—or an interplay of yin and yang. The yang was the active, aggressive striking force—the assertive male energy—and the yin, yielding, receptive, passive, feminine.

The philosopher observed the yin was stronger than the yang. For when the snake had tired itself from too many strikes, too much exertion, the stork struck, impaling the snake on its beak.

When we are confronted by anger, pain, or hostility from another, our tendency is to "strike back" with an equally assertive force—to meet yang (male) with yang (male)—however this seldom works, and only escalates the tension.

When you are centered, you can be "yin" (feminine)—or water—and allow the person to vent their feelings. When they are through you will know how they are feeling, and be able to respond appropriately.

Development of this "water" energy will occur rapidly if you have a willingness to go into parts of your-self that you have never explored; a willingness to be vulnerable, to risk feelings, to risk being you, and then to act on that inner knowing. From that deep, inner place comes a communication that speaks without words.

It is a well-known axiom that you can't help someone else beyond your own point of inner clarity. When I first started working with cancer patients, the physical and emotional pain of the dying patients was too much for me. At the end of the first day, I literally threw up when I got home. I had to "clear up" my own stuff before I could go on. Whenever we are trying to help, understand, or listen to another, we must first deal with whatever emotions or reactions get triggered in us before "listening" can take place at a deeper level.

The first cancer patient that I helped move toward death was a woman named Maria. She was in the very advanced stages of her illness. I was with Maria almost constantly during her last few days and during that time, I asked her, "Maria, how can I help you?"

"Just love me," she said, "and pray for me."

She needed me to listen to her in a way that communicated caring. No words were necessary, just a sensitivity and willingness to be there.

Receptivity means not having to always fill space with talk and chatter. Communication isn't always verbal. In fact, it can get in the way, preventing a deeper sharing.

As I sat with Maria, I learned to get beyond my need to keep her mind (and mine) preoccupied with pleasantry. There is great power in the pause, knowing when to be silent, when to speak, when to leave someone alone, when to allow others in—and when to make time for yourself, pausing in the day to be quiet. To be still—and to know.

Invoking The Water Element

EXERCISE FOR DEVELOPING RECEPTIVITY

1. To develop the power of Water, two qualities are absolutely necessary: Respect and Openness.

In every situation, with any individual, always assume that they deserve your respect, have a valid point, and need to be heard. Live in the spirit of this affirmation: I want to understand you, and I want you to understand me.

2. To develop the quality of openness, be attentive, and listen without interruption.

If a person makes a statement, don't assume you understand what they mean. Rephrase what you think you heard by asking:

"Are you saying. . .?" Or, "This is what I think I heard you say. . .Am I correct?"

Other types of "water" questions can be:

"How do you see this working out?"

"What would you like to see happen?"

"Does that mean...?"

"How can I support you?"

To develop the power of "water," you need to be very fluid and not afraid of the unknown. If you are open, you can draw out a person. If you think you know everything about a person or situation, then you already have established limits on the relationship or the communication. But if you are curious and have developed a quality of openness, then you are able to drop your defenses and flow with the situation, expanding the possibilities in the relationship or the communication.

EXPERIENCE TO DEVELOP RECEPTIVITY: FOR PARTNERS

Do this exercise with a good friend, someone you are comfortable with. Begin by sitting face to face. Be still for a few moments and then take turns, saying to each other, "I want to understand you, and I want you to understand me."

Partner (A) says:

"Please give me your insights on any situation that you are aware of that isn't working in my life." (such as: How I deal with my child; Why I am confused about...; The problem I am having with....)

Partner (A) listens while Partner (B) gives her insights and feelings on where there are blocks.

(A) listens, respecting the other's observations, making no comments, excuses, apologies, nor offering explanations or rationalizations. When (B) has finished, (A) can now ask questions such as:

"Are you saying that...?"

"What else have you noticed...?"

"What else did you feel when you saw (or heard

about) me doing that?"

"How do you think I could have done that differently?"

There should be no attempt to justify. Simply be respectful and open about your partner's point of view. Ask the type of questions that help clarify the communication, and listen for as long as it takes.

(A) thanks her partner and spends some time sharing thoughts and feelings about the input. (B) is allowed to respond again. The process continues until it feels complete. Listening without defense is the first step in developing receptivity.

The partners reverse roles and start over.

Element Air

The energy within us that is
COMMUNICATIVE, CLEAR, LIGHT, JOYOUS,
HUMOROUS, SPONTANEOUS, CREATIVE

At a traumatic time in my life, I called Suzzane, my seventy-year-young friend, for consolation and advice. My husband and I had just separated. I was moving out of the area, and I was in a panic. Suzzane was my "guardian angel," someone I turned to often in times of uncertainty and distress. Naturally, I counted on her to be sympathetic and to give me some good advice, perhaps even to invite me to New York to spend a few days together and talk.

"Suzzane," I said, struggling with waves of desperation and self-pity, "I don't know what I'm going to do or where I'm going to live." There was a brief pause on the other end of the line, and then, bubbling with her characteristic joy for life, she replied. "Oh, how exciting! I'll have to try that sometime."

Her quick comeback startled me. It wasn't what I

expected. But it broke through my wall of confusion. Truly, "angels" are beings that take things lightly. Instead of crying on her shoulder, as I had imagined, we began laughing together. Her "lightness," her spontaneity took all the heaviness out of the situation and transformed it. I began to see the challenges, the possibilities of my situation with a renewed spirit and hope. My self-pity was a substitute for self-love.

Air Changes Perspectives

In Native American tradition, the Grandfather of the East is represented by the eagle. The East is the direction of the sunrise, where light first appears. The Grandfather of the East is the spirit of new beginnings, new insight. Of all winged creatures, the eagle soars higher than any other, and thus represents heightened perception, the eye that encompasses all the possibilities. It is the spirit of the Air.

The energy and power of the "air" element is the energy of communication and clarity. Air gives us the ability to see joy and opportunity in the challenge of life's experiences. And it contains an almost child-like quality of trust, wonder, excitement, expectancy, and play.

Flooded By Water, Rescued By Air

Once, when I was scheduled to do a Mediation Training workshop for the Association for Research & Enlightenment, Inc. (A.R.E.) in Virginia Beach, I had an unforgettable experience with the magical quality of the "air" energy. I had flown in from Texas the day before and had one day to prepare before the scheduled workshop. Mediation is a very effective form of conflict resolution, and in the past, I had given the Mediation Training with Russell, an attorney friend. For our workshops, we used the Thomas-Killman Conflict Mode test. We had purchased them jointly, and Russell stored the unused tests in his office.

When I called Russell to get the tests, I discovered from his partner, Douglas, that Russell was out of town. I told Douglas what I needed and why, and said I would come right by to pick them up. I didn't see any problem and expected a quick, uncomplicated response like, "Sure, come on by." Instead I got an abrupt, "I can't possibly give you those tests without Russell's permission." My stomach did a flip flop. I suddenly felt like I stepped on a snake! "Oh, but you don't understand," I implored. "I am counting on those tests. Russell and I have been friends for twenty years. Those tests belong to both of us. We bought them together."

But he was unmoved. "Before I can release anything from this office, I need to have Russell's permission." The voice sounded precise and authoritarian. "As far as I am concerned, you are just like any woman off the street." I was too startled to respond.

"Do you have a problem with calling Russell?" the voice asked. Of course I did! Russell was somewhere in North Carolina on a holiday, and the chances of reaching him were slim. I was getting angry, and struggling with feelings of panic and frustration. In the confusion, my Pleasing Passive stepped out of the closet.

"Do you have a number where I can reach him?" I asked weakly. Actually, I was much too "emerged" to blow up. Instead, I scribbled down the number as he recited it to me, and when I called, I got to hear the phone ring and ring and ring. No one was there.

The whole situation seemed stupid, hopeless, and unnecessary! I had two options. I could call him back and plead some more—or really give him a piece of my mind! And neither one would have gotten me what I wanted.

"So, how can I turn this situation around?" I thought. The answer came quickly. "Invoke the Air. Change your perspective!" And suddenly instead of it being a hopeless deadlock, the situation became a challenge to my creativity!

I changed my focus and looked at the situation through Douglas's eyes. He is a logical, systematic, orderly thinker. He is in charge of the office. It's Saturday and he's catching up on his own work and doesn't want to be bothered. Obviously my attempt to appeal to Doug's feelings wouldn't work. If I got angry, he'd just get defensive. The task then is how can I communicate to a left-brain lawyer in a way that he can relate to.

Obviously, Doug was very much an "earth" energy, and I am "water." My normal way of relating is through feelings and emotion, his through logic and reason. I could bathe him in a flood of water energy, and Doug would simply build a dam and pull out a towel. Or we would make a lot of mud.

I needed Air to get above the impasse. After a few minutes, I called back with a new perspective.

"Douglas, I really appreciate the fact that you are being responsible with the office. I haven't been able to reach Russell yet. How would it be if I came to the office and signed an affidavit stating that I have taken the tests? That way you'll be protected."

"No, that won't be necessary," he replied cordially. Obviously a woman who thought that way was a reasonable person. Now I was someone he could relate to. The whole energy changed, and instead of a clash, it became a dance.

"You see, the real problem is," he said, "I don't know where the tests are—and I don't want to go look for them."

"I am pretty sure I know where they are. Do you mind checking?"

He said he didn't, so I described where I thought they were, and he went and hunted for them—but without any success.

"I'm sorry," he said, "but the tests aren't there." And then Douglas volunteered a welcomed suggestion. "Why don't you keep trying to get Russell? If you can find out where the tests are, call me back, and I'll bring the tests to you when I leave today." The entire situation had been transformed through the openness of Air.

***

"Nobody does anything deliberately in the interest of evil, for the sake of evil. Everyone acts in the interest of good as he understands it and everyone understands it in a different way." (Author unknown)

***

Other Perspectives

In this age of the liberated woman, many women still get despondent because they are alone or without a man. If we fail to see the challenge and possibilities in the opportunity of being alone, being on our own can be a very "heavy" experience. Or it can be a time of great opportunity.

"Honey, there's a whole lot of things worse than being single—and being able to do what you want to do!" observed one woman, with years of wisdom and homespun humor, to a depressed, young, single woman at a workshop in California.

The energy and power of air is lightheartedness. No wonder that this quality of Spirit is often depicted in fairy tales as a free-spirited elf, Puckish sprite, or angel. But most of all, having the element of air means never losing the joyous curiosity and excitement about life.

With the element of air, we can lift ourselves from the weariness and burdens of a situation to experience the joy and lightness present in almost every moment!

Take It Off, Mama!

I was once walking down Madison Avenue in Manhattan during the rush hour when suddenly I felt a tapping on my shoulder. I turned to see a lady who I assumed had mistaken me for someone else. I smiled and kept walking. A few steps later, the lady tapped on my shoulder again, this time with greater insistence. When I turned to face her, she seemed very embarrassed and pointed with great urgency to the sidewalk. I looked down at my feet, thinking I was being warned about a manhole or a pile of dog droppings. What was it? I didn't see anything. Again, she pointed insistently toward the ground—toward my feet. The look on her face was one of alarm.

Peeping out from beneath the hem of my left trouser was an inch or two of bright blue panty hose. I had worn the slacks the day before and apparently, in my rush to get undressed I had taken off the slacks, hose and all. And the hose had stayed tucked in the leg. Now they were inching their way down my leg and dragging under my shoe!

What could I do? I couldn't just stand there cross-legged and smile. There was no convenient place to change. And every time I took another step, a little more of the panty hose crept out from the leg.

A few years earlier I would have withered in shame and embarrassment. But I realized that wouldn't do any good. I made a decision. Since the situation couldn't be ignored, why not really get into it and enjoy it? Quite suddenly the Puckish spirit of Air possessed me. Instead of surreptitiously sneaking it off my leg I reached down and started to pull the hose from my pants leg in an overly exaggerated flamboyant gesture. At this point a small crowd started to gather. Now the thing about panty hose is, the more you pull, the more there is to pull. It is like taffy. It just keeps stretching and stretching. At this point, two of the most handsome men I had ever seen turned the corner and came walking past me. I smiled sheepishly as if to say, No, I don't do this often, just every now and then. Someone in the crowd hollered, "Take it off, Mama!" By now I was pulling out the last inch of panty hose, twirling it high above my head, and cracking it like a whip. I bent toward the two newcomers with an exaggerated bow and stuffed my hose back into my purse. The small crowd which had gathered around burst into applause and laughter. The two delighted men asked if I was going to disrobe any further. When I assured them I wasn't, they good naturedly invited me to have lunch which, unfortunately, I had to decline. It was great fun while it lasted. Had it occurred a year or two earlier, it would have been a mortal blow to my ego.

Yes, Angels are beings that take things lightly.

Exercise For The Element Of Air

The best place to get in touch with the element of air is in the mountains, where the air is fresh and pure. Spend time alone, walking the hills or on mountain trails. It's one of the best ways to change your perspective and to revitalize yourself.

If no hills or mountains are available, find a special place you can go to be all alone, and just notice how the breeze feels blowing through your hair, or caressing your face. You can go to a physical location, or simply do it in your imagination, as a reverie. Notice how the wind can soothe your thoughts and calm your mind. We are enveloped in air. Become one with the "air." Experience its joy and lightness. Allow the soft, soothing motion of the air to breathe lightness into your thoughts and freedom into your spirit.

Element Fire

The energy within us that is
COURAGE, DETERMINATION, POWER, PASSION, ENERGY, CONVICTION, INSPIRATION, CREATIVITY

"Naomi, would you like to take charge of this committee?"

The conference committee chairman looked hopefully toward the handsome black woman. Naomi was a natural leader, calm, confident and experienced—someone all the others looked to and relied upon. Naomi smiled easily. "Why no, I don't believe so." She responded with such equanimity and self-assurance that, at first, it felt as if she had accepted. Did she say yes or did she say no?

Coming from Naomi, "Why no, I don't believe so," sounded like a melody. Her words carried no guilt whatsoever. No explanations, no justification, just self-confidence.

The Last To Be Claimed

The Grandfather of the South is the spirit of fire, passion, love, and vitality. It is the direction of the summer, the season of abundance, growth, and fullness. This Grandfather governs the processes of life and death, birth and rebirth.

Fire is usually the last element that a woman claims. It is the power to take action, to be decisive, to make decisions. And most women have been trained to give that power to others.

In claiming our fire, we need to learn the creative use of two very important words, YES and NO. There is incredible magic in these words.

The "creative no" and the "gracious yes" are two sides of the same coin. We need to be able to say both with ease. Naomi is someone who says "yes" to a lot of things in life. But like her, we can all benefit by learning to say "no" to the false demands on our time, to the relationship which is not working, and to say "yes" to ourselves, to our lives—to giving and living. Fire is released through a decision to act. Once we know in our heart what the right thing is to do, if we commit to that course of action, it seems as if the energy of life will come to our aid. Energy follows action!

Recently I had the pleasure and satisfaction of hosting a small party to celebrate a milestone in the life of my friend, Janet—the obtaining of her Master's degree. It was a triumph of fire! After many years away from school, Janet became convinced it was important for her to complete her graduate degree. At the time, she had no idea how to finance her tuition or how she would support herself while completing the two-year program. But the time was right, and she took the first step, applied for admission, and was accepted. Then, quite unexpectedly, her parents offered financial support. In her second year, she received another unexpected gift from someone else who wanted to support her in her career choice.

One of the joys of that party was listening to Janet recount these and other little stories about how things kept working out for her—the unexpected new car, timely help from friends and family—to support her in her decision and commitments.

Because she was bold enough to believe in what she wanted to do, and made a commitment to it, other things came that supported her in the decision. Had she waited for the right time and conditions to appear before making that commitment, she would still be waiting.

Many women have issues about making decisions, and they opt to remain in a state of confusion for months, even years—perhaps a lifetime. Confusion is a condition that results from not wanting to be responsible for choices. We play it safe. We can't be certain what the results of our actions might be. So we take no action. And we remain in confusion.

Many women also live waiting for lightning to strike. They seem to think, "When the bolt flashes, when the light hits—then I'll be clear. Then I'll know what to do." But life can't be lived fully waiting for something to happen. We have to make the choice to "release our fire," and then the energy follows. We must take the first step, even if we don't know exactly where the next one will take us. If we find out later we went down the wrong road, or missed the right path, then we can always make another choice, and choose to move in another direction.

"Life, you are too beautiful for us to realize!" The words of Thornton Wilder from *Our Town* always come back to remind us how much we hold back on life, resisting and hesitating because of the fear of the unknown.

There is not a better story about "claiming your fire" than the one about young Michelangelo.

Because of his enormous talent, Michelangelo was selected to enter the School of the Medici. The young artist was thrilled to be studying with the great masters. Each day, Michelangelo would draw laboriously, And each day, his teachers would pick up his drawings without comment—neither criticism nor praise.

This practice continued for many months, until more than a year had passed. Other students advanced into other media—pastels, textile, paint, and a few of the most gifted began working with stone, which was

Michelangelo's passion. Still, Michelangelo was only permitted to draw. And his drawings continued to be unceremoniously collected without comment by his teachers.

Finally, Michelangelo could stand it no longer. Though it was forbidden, he stole into the Medici quarry under cover of darkness, armed with his sculpting tools. His heart pounding with excitement, he selected a choice piece of marble, and began sculpturing. From the lifeless stone, the curves and outlines of a magnificent stallion started to emerge.

The next day, an exhausted but exhilarated Michelangelo was confronted by his teacher on the way to class.

"Buonarroti," the stern-faced master asked, "Is it true? Did you enter the quarry last night and defile the stone without permission?"

"I did," the young artist confessed.

"Then go to the Medici immediately," the instructor ordered.

The students all knew the rules. With such a flagrant violation, expulsion seemed inevitable.

The Medici was one of the most feared and powerful men of his time. Michelangelo trembled as he walked down the long corridor to the office, where the Medici waited for him.

"Michael, is it true that you entered the quarry illegally last night without permission of the school and defiled stone?" the imposing figure behind the desk asked him.

"Yes," Michelangelo answered, "I did."

Without a further word, the Medici reached into his desk and pulled out a large leather folder. It was Michelangelo's portfolio with every drawing he had ever done at the school.

The Master Medici laid the drawings on the desk

and looked at them with great admiration. Then he looked up at Michelangelo, and said, "We always knew you had the talent, but we didn't know if you had the courage. Go, the quarry is yours."

Michelangelo had genius. And he had fire—the courage and passion to follow his heart!

Exercise For Claiming Your Fire

Learning to make clear decisions and stick with them is an important key to claiming your fire. Remember, we can never have all the facts sufficient for making the right decision. We can never be guaranteed that our decision will have the results we hope for. But what we can do is make the best decision we are capable of, based on a combination of facts and intuition. We can weigh what we know about a situation (the facts) with the way we feel about it (our intuition) and then make a decision, giving equal importance to both.

CLAIM YOUR FIRE

1. State a decision, or course of action to a pressing, immediate, or real situation present in your life, based upon everything you know and feel about the situation you are addressing.

On a sheet of paper write out what seems like your best option. Write it as a letter to yourself, affirming that unless you find some reason to change your mind in the next twenty-four hours, this is what you will do.

2. Wait for twenty-four hours. During that time, look for signs, symbols, any meaningful "synchronicity" that may either confirm or alter your decision. If nothing happens to change your mind, act on your decision.

Don't hold back or look back. Claim your fire, and

move forward! Jump in. Energy will follow action!

Ritual For Transforming
False Power To Real Power

This is an exercise for calling upon the earth, water, air, and fire elements and for transforming the Bitch. It can be effective done alone, or with a group for added power. It is a ritual to consciously awaken your awareness of your ability to transform and to mark in your mind an important event. It is the moment of deciding that you do have a choice and that you are a creator of your own reality.

Step 1. Name The Bitch
Refer to the chart at the end of Chapter One. Which of these Bitches can you identify with? You may relate to several or identify with many, but select one, preferably the one that you use most often.

When you have identified the Bitch that you want to transform, write her name down on a small slip of paper and fold it in half.

Step 2. Dismiss Her False Power
Acknowledge that you alone have created this Bitch, that you know her name, that she exists within you, and that you can accept her. Affirm that you no longer want this false power to dominate your life.

Step 3. Replace False Power With Real Power
Be silent for a moment and acknowledge the Higher Power that is within you. Choose the element that is most needed to bring you into wholeness. Invoke the spirit of the elements to awaken that greater part of yourself. For example, if you are the Pleasing Passive, you may need to call forth "fire" and evoke the qualities of taking action, speaking out, and saying "no" to the things that don't work for you. Or, if you are a Mother

Superior, you may want to call forth the element of water and the quality of listening, of being open, receptive, and curious to others. Let your mind be inventive, creative, and resourceful in creating this experience.

Step 4. Affirm Your Power. It Is Done.

Using a candle, fireplace, hibachi, or whatever is suitable, create a ceremony to mark the dismissal of the Bitch. As you call forth the powers of transformation, hold or drop the paper with the name of your Bitch into the flame. The flame represents the power of transformation and purification. Verbally say, "I dismiss (name the Bitch), and call forth instead (name the energy and its qualities).

Example: "I dismiss the Shrieking War Goddess and call forth "water" and that ability within me to be curious about others and their opinions and to listen with an open heart."

Now, know in your heart that it is done.

The ceremony does not mean that the Shrieking War Goddess will never appear again in your life. But as soon as she does, you can quickly recognize her presence and dismiss her. Then confidently choose other options—earth, water, air, fire, or one of the Goddesses that you will meet in the next chapter.

Be aware that you will be challenged by your Bitch time and time again. They don't die easily. But once you know the process for dismissing her false power, whenever you feel her arise, you can quickly go through these steps in your mind and, in time, achieve complete mastery. Ultimately you might even smile or be amused when you feel her raise her ugly head. Then, with inner confidence, gracefully and quickly, dismiss her as you choose a more appropriate and fulfilling response.

The pantheon of Greek goddesses reflects the diversity and complexity within women and provides us with a new way of looking at ourselves from a perspective which is thoroughly feminine. Of all the myths and folktales, the goddesses of the Greeks are drawn with the greatest clarity and light about them. We look to them as containing the great archetypal principles of the feminine. Until very recently, these archetypes have been lost to Western culture due to the devaluation of the feminine principle. As women, we need the association with these great powerful archetypes. As we awaken and search for wholeness, the goddesses return to help us in our journey.

CHAPTER 5

Awakening The Goddess

Sundays were family day for our clan, and included a ritual that I particularly treasured. Dad and Mom and we four children would dress up in our Sunday best, get the final check and nod of approval from Mom, and then we'd walk out the door and down the street two blocks to the red brick church on the corner.

The Baptist church was a comforting sight to me, though it was something of an architectural nightmare. The music was always heartfelt and slightly off-key. The church suppers with good potato salad and the crusty apple pies were delicious and ample. And the warm handshakes, the open hearts, and the accepting smiles created a feeling of belonging.

I still can remember sitting on the stiff wooden benches during the church service, waiting for the sermon to end. I would watch the hands of the church clock turn ever so slowly, while my mother stared down at me from the choir loft with an unnerving look designed to keep my squirming and whispers to a minimum.

We would linger after the service, talking to friends, and then the family would head home for a Sunday feast of roast beef or baked hen served on a beautifully set table with white linen, fine silver, and fresh flowers. We took turns blessing the food, and then with great admiration, we'd watch Dad roll up his sleeves, sharpen the carving knife with a flair, and skillfully slice the meat for our special meal.

Though I loved the fellowship of the Baptist Church, there was still something missing. My mother was rather ecumenical in her approach, so I had little trouble getting permission to visit other church services, which I often did after Sunday school. I was particularly fond of the Methodist service. But it didn't satisfy my curiosity, and in due time, I visited every church in town. The only real taboo for a Baptist was Catholicism. So, naturally, I was fascinated by that, too.

I had a Catholic friend named Georgianna. One night when I was visiting, her mother called her to join the family for evening prayers. From the room upstairs, I could hear,

"Hail Mary, Full of Grace, The Lord is with thee, blessed art thou among women."

I was nine years old at the time, and it was one of those moments I shall never forget. There was a power in those words, and a deep sense of serenity and peace. A comforting presence seemed to reach out and envelop me. It was a prayer to a woman. Was God a mother, too? The Baptists and the Methodists only talked about Jesus, gentle, meek, and mild, and the powerful, strong God of the Old Testament—the God of Abraham, Isaac, and Jacob.

The next week, quite unexpectedly, I came across a discarded catechism in the lost-and-found of my aunt's movie theater. It had been there for weeks, and she was about to throw it out. Meekly, I asked if I could have it. With some hesitation, she agreed. I couldn't believe it. I had a catechism—and it had been given to me by my strict Baptist aunt. That seemed like a miracle in itself!

I quickly memorized every word of the book,

including the Hail Mary invocation. The following Sunday, I attended Catholic mass and continued going to mass for several months, until on one sticky, sultry summer day, I passed out, overcome with the smell of incense during a *Bendectus* service. To make matters worse, a Catholic family whom I didn't even know was delegated to drive me home. When my father discovered where I had been, he forbade me to continue going to the Catholic church. It was out of the question! For a nine-year-old girl to go to mass by herself was absurd, especially when her father was Protestant, and staunchly Baptist at that!

My affinity for Mary continued unabated, though it had to go underground. I no longer attended the Catholic mass, but I continued praying the *Hail Mary* whenever I sought peace and stillness.

And the concept of Mary, the Mother of God, has expanded in scope and richness through the years. As a child, I felt her presence through my *Hail Marys.* In other cultures and others times, I would have called to her with other names—Isis, Ashtar, Sophia, Kwan Yin—and her compassionate heart would have opened to me. It is as though Mary connected me to a deep memory of another time when woman and femininity was far better understood than now.

Through Mary, I began my search for that feminine aspect of the Divine, and from that awakening has grown a deep, inner realization of the gentleness and strength that is a woman.

A Palette of Colors

As women, we have options and choices. It is rather like discovering that we have a beautiful palette of colors at our disposal, and we can graciously and skillfully choose which color or combination of colors are appropriate in any given circumstance or situation. Too often we paint our canvas of life with just a few familiar, tried-and-true colors, when there is an infinite range of shades, textures, and tones available. Why limit ourselves, when we can create a masterpiece!

In the previous chapter we were introduced to the four elements and several exercises were offered to help us identify and work with the essence or value of these energies in our daily life. The seven goddesses of this chapter are here to help awaken, activate, and direct the other qualities or aspects of ourselves that have been dormant. To claim the goddesses, we need only call their name and remember their qualities. As we discover their presence, we can bring them forth. The more conscious we become, the more magic we can create.

In this chapter, we will be introduced to the seven goddesses of Greek mythology. In the first Emerging Woman workshops I co-taught with a good friend, Carol Ann Bush, a licensed Guided Imagery and Music (GIM) therapist, we introduced five goddesses. Later, we increased the goddesses to seven. When Jean Shinoda Bolen's book, *Goddesses in Everywoman,* came out, we were quite surprised—and delighted—to discover she included the same seven archetypes. Synchronicity is amazing!

Because it is the definitive work on the subject, I recommend you read *Goddesses in Everywoman* and use it as a reference book for understanding the goddess archetypes. The focus of this chapter is to offer a brief sketch of each goddess, and to offer experiential techniques for activating the goddess energies within.

Just as the four elements describe qualities that can be best expressed through symbols, the goddess images offer us ways of getting in touch with other dimensions of the inner self that are felt or sensed, but not easily articulated. Each one represents a distinctly feminine pattern. As women, we all carry one or more of those patterns, or archetypes, within us.

*　*　*

Ritual, symbol, and ceremony are important parts of our spiritual journey. Women respond to symbols, ritual, and other images of feminine wholeness because what we feel connected to most deeply, or intuitively, is not easily expressed through words.

*　*　*

"Archetype" is a Jungian term for patterns that form the strong inner forces which are in us all. They are inherent in our very nature, even though we may not be fully conscious of them. When we look at the archetype represented by the goddesses and see their form as the ancients visualized them, we have a reference point to understand what is alive, what is latent, what is dormant, and what is active within our feminine power. The goddesses can be allies—or obstacles, for each goddess has a negative as well as positive side. When we can "name" the goddess, we can claim the power and support she offers.

As archetypes, the goddesses expand our concept of what is feminine. As a pantheon, they contain and express all the qualities we label either "masculine" or "feminine." Instead of being limited to one or two cultural role models for what it means to be a woman, the goddesses present us with a range of options and a myriad of examples of how to express different energies. As you read through this pantheon of goddesses, be aware that in different stages of your life, different archetypes may be awakened and emerge.

In early adolescence, when all the hormones go to work, and a girl goes "boy crazy," Aphrodite may emerge. For a new mother, holding the helpless, newborn child to her bosom will awaken Demeter. Later in life, when some women experience the "empty nest" syndrome, the Athena or Artemis archetype may get activated. Margaret Mead calls it PMZ—post menstrual zest. These are the women who go back to school, take on a job, or pursue a new career. It initiates the zenith of their life. The Hera archetype may wonder what all the fuss is about for she much prefers to stay by her partner's side. But for a woman who has a strong Persephone component, this time of life can be devastating. She may be desperately clinging to youth, hesitant to claim the joy of the maturing woman.

The most interesting thing about identifying with these goddesses is that, though each of us normally have one dominant archetype, the more conscious we become, the more archetypes we can awaken.

It's natural. Our child comes into the room, the Demeter "Earth Mother" is aroused. We go back to our desk and work on our checkbook and invoke the practicality and wisdom of an Athena consciousness. The phone rings and a friend has a problem, we bring forth Hestia, the all-wise woman, listening, counseling. We have it all within us.

As you read this chapter, be aware of which of the goddess patterns you identify with. And which do you need to invoke to become more whole? There is power in "naming the name" to invoke, direct, or control an energy. We can all do it. How simple and uncomplicated it was as children to become whatever we focused on as we played—hero, queen, "Wonder Woman," Cinderella, Florence Nightingale, doctor, lawyer, astronaut. As children, we did this naturally. As adults, we have to re-learn it. The same principal applies here. The energy can be summoned by knowing its name.

As we open to the possibilities of becoming empowered by the strength of our femininity, we realize that there is more to being a woman than we ever may have imagined.

The Virginal Goddesses

Artemis, Athena, Hestia

The Virginal Goddesses are self-contained. They do not necessarily have to be in a relationship or partnership with a male to be complete. Virginal in this sense doesn't necessarily mean chaste. It connotes that they are their own person, rather than needing to belong to another.

Artemis—Goddess of Direction

VITAL, QUICK MOVING, UNBOUNDED, FOCUSED, FREE, FIERCE, WISE, PSYCHIC, INDEPENDENT, BOLD, ATHLETIC, DETERMINED

Artemis is a woman of enormous energy and vigor. She is portrayed as the goddess of the hunt, wearing a tunic and carrying a silver bow. The goddess of wild things, nature, and vitality, she rejoices in the quest and loves to live life at its edges. There is a sense of great freedom around her. Don't ever try to tell her what to do!

Today, she can be found in the young woman dressed in blue jeans and a back pack. She loves nature and is an explorer of unknown places, both within herself and without. The goddess of the moon, Artemis loves quiet and solitude and goes deeply into things. She stays naturally attuned to her inner self. Her wisdom grows from her independent nature, and her aloneness. Known as the goddess of sisterhood, her primary friendships are with females. She may have a number of encounters with men, but more as an adventure, rather than as a committed relationship.

A negative Artemis can be too cold and may tend to spurn close male relationships. Her fear is of becoming too closely connected and losing her freedom.

THE SPIRIT OF ARTEMIS

Once a woman with a strong Artemis energy came to visit me from Holland. We were walking along on a public beach. The weather was quite chilly—about forty-five degrees—and a few strollers were bundled up and leaning against the wind. Suddenly, spontaneously, this Artemis stripped to the buff and dove into the waves. Meanwhile, I and the other passers-by watched in amazement. I shivered just looking at her. After a few minutes, she came out totally refreshed by her swim, dressed, and we continued our walk down the beach.

Another Artemis woman spent an entire college semester happily planting trees twelve hours a day, the only female in a class of men. She loved every minute of it. The Artemis woman is quite happy with calluses on her hands and a little soil on her jeans.

Athena—Goddess of Consciousness

TALL, GRACEFUL, EXPRESSIVE, BALANCED, INNOVATIVE, PRACTICAL, WISE, SHREWD, VISIONARY—A LEADER, A CRAFTSWOMAN

Athena is a magnificent woman, the giver of courage and talent. Clarity of mind, wisdom, and innovative ideas are her prominent attributes. The goddess of creativity, culture, and consciousness, she loves to initiate ideas and can orchestrate things. She is a craftswoman, a weaver who understands how things fit together. She is the energy that motivates, the voice that speaks, "Come on, let's get going!" She won't let you get stuck in dark places. A visionary, Athena doesn't like to deal with petty things. Her interest is piqued by subjects of great importance. If there is a man in her life, he is usually a mentor or teacher to her. She doesn't relate to weak men. Instead, she wants someone else to match her own power. At the same time, Athena can help awaken a man's own heroic capacity.

Perhaps her greatest quality is that she can really be out front, voicing what needs to be said or expressed. She speaks for many, a spokeswoman for the collective.

A negative Athena can get too involved in her mission. She loses her softness. Concern for her body and her gentleness take a back seat, and she can become too tough.

THE SPIRIT OF ATHENA

Athena was born "out of the head" of Zeus. She is, definitely, her father's daughter, intensely loyal to him and to the powerful men in her life. In the Roman myth, when Arachne dared to weave a tapestry which revealed the indiscretions of Zeus, Minerva (the Roman counterpart of Athena) tore it up and turned Arachne into a spider so that she would be more careful about what designs she wove in the future. Though Zeus's indiscretions are known to everyone, Minerva is stubbornly loyal. It didn't matter that Arachne's tapestry depicted the truth!

Bella Abzug, Indira Ghandi, Margaret Thatcher are all Athena women. Perhaps the most archetypal Athena today is Shirley MacLaine. Shirley has a visionary view of life and has made public her beliefs and experiences with the Higher Mind, while putting her reputation and career "out on a limb." She has opened new horizons and speaks for many. She is a spokeswoman for higher consciousness in our time.

Hestia—Goddess Of The Hearthfire

SERENE, INWARD, PEACEFUL, HARMONIOUS, SERVING, WISE, CONTAINED, HEALING, UNDERSTANDING, DEEP

In the myths, there is no exact form assigned to Hestia. And there is a good reason for that. Hestia is felt more as a presence. She is the wise, intuitive old woman. Her wisdom comes from experience and inner peace. She is a woman who values simple tasks. If you find her in the kitchen baking bread, she is humming contentedly. There is a calm rhythm to her life, a softness, a flow.

Though she might marry, the Hestia woman enjoys solitude and has not the slightest concern for name, status, or fame. She creates confidence in others, she gives kindness, she is thoughtful and considerate. She needs no words to communicate her understanding of life. You can feel it just being with her. This quality can be transforming. To reach that kind of depth takes years of inner development.

Because of her inner peace, her negative traits are few, *if any.* A negative Hestia may get so caught up in her solitude that she doesn't do enough for herself. She may not enter into life enough to fully experience it. If she becomes too withdrawn and isolated or content in her peace, she may not reach out at a time when she needs to.

THE SPIRIT OF HESTIA

Once I had a minor acting role in an amateur theater version of *The Sound of Music*. To make certain our costumes were authentic, we asked several nuns to come and help us dress properly in our habits. The nun that helped me with my costume had incredible eyes. When she looked at me, I felt she was seeing to the bottom of my toes. She communicated a feeling of love and peace through her eyes, the windows of the soul.

On the global scale, Mother Theresa is the embodiment of Hestia. Mother Theresa is deeply attuned to the depths of the feminine spirit, so in tune with it that she receives direct guidance from the Holy Mother. Once when the civil war was raging in Lebanon, she asked the authorities for permission to go in and rescue the damaged and forgotten children. The authorities told her it was impossible to go in unless there was a ceasefire, and the possibility of that happening was very remote. "That was fine," Mother Theresa responded. The Holy Mother Mary had told her there would be a ceasefire the next day—and there was!

The Vulnerable Goddesses

Hera, Demeter, Persephone

These goddesses are not self-contained. They need to be in a relationship to be complete.

Hera—Goddess Of Loyalty

MATRIARCH, COMMITTED, STEADFAST, QUARRELSOME, POSSESSIVE, LEGALISTIC, TALENTED, RESPONSIBLE

Hera is a powerful archetype. A devoted partner to her husband and often the power behind the throne, Hera teaches us about what it is to be committed to a relationship. You can always count on a Hera archetype to do what she says. She's very responsible and carries out her work. Many institutions, schools, churches, and hospitals would be lost without her.

Hera would never think of identifying herself as Ms. She is a Mrs., and it is not a sacrifice to submerge her individuality and totally identify with her husband's name and family. She is a pillar of strength and dependability and can nurture creative offspring.

Negative Hera can be unyielding, rigid, quarrel-some, and legalistic. Woe to the person who crosses her husband! She is totally loyal, and very jealous.

Some women, when thrust into a Hera role, find it devastating. They can't quite "cut it," and it drives them to depression, drugs, or alcohol. And woe to the Hera woman who discovers her husband has been unfaithful or wants out of the marriage. Such news could be totally devastating for her identity is dependent too much on him. The pressure to be "Mrs. *Somebody*" can be fierce!

THE SPIRIT OF HERA

Jean is a diplomat's wife. She developed cancer when they were at a post in Africa. She had to go to England for surgery, and her husband was not able to come to the hospital because of his schedule and responsibilities. At the time, she accepted his not being there to support her. Her identity was so connected to her role as the supportive wife that she believed her personal feelings and needs didn't count. Her husband's career was all-important. Years later, when the cancer reappeared, she finally got in touch with her rage at being assigned a low priority in his life.

Demeter—The Earth Mother Goddess

ABUNDANCE, PROSPERITY, NURTURING, CARING, COMPASSIONATE, FEELING, GROUNDED, STRONG, DEVOTED, POSSESSIVE, PROTECTIVE

In the myths, Demeter is celebrated as the mother who would not cease grieving until she recovered her lost daughter. She goes to any length to retrieve her, even entering into the Underworld. For Demeter, life is not centered in her man, but in her children—or whomever she claims as her child. Her main power is to give birth and to nourish. In regard to her children (whether they be her own flesh and blood, or students, patients, *etc.*), Demeter's creativity is enormous. Her nurturing and caring is special. She knows when to hold a hand, fluff a pillow, and when to step in and take action. She has a flawless intuition; her timing is perfect. She has a natural ability to accept a child as he or she is, which gives them an enormous self-confidence. She loves them as they are. It's the most empowering gift of all!

Demeter women are often in the helping professions, as nurses, midwives, teachers, and counselors. They understand the cycles of life and death very well, and can assist people as they pass through the entrance and the exit doors of life. Demeter applies her nurturing qualities in the workplace. This often makes retirement emotionally difficult for her.

For a negative Demeter, the hardest thing is to let go of her children, whoever they might be. "What's the matter with my son? He hasn't called today! He and his wife should come to my home for Sunday dinner." And on it goes!

THE SPIRIT OF DEMETER

Once I had the privilege of visiting the St. Christopher's Hospice, outside London, England's first experiment with hospice care. The woman who gave us the tour that day was a delight. She had big hips, big bosoms, and a broad, genuine smile. Her face was peaceful, her eyes and spirit serene and loving. It felt safe just being with her. When I die, I thought, how comforting to be with someone like her.

Persephone—Goddess Of The Subconscious

YOUTHFUL, OPEN, RECEPTIVE, YIELDING, INDECISIVE, VULNERABLE, SINCERE, UNSURE, TRUSTING, MYSTICAL, POWERFUL, UNDERSTANDING

Persephone is the daughter of Demeter. She is the youthful maiden who can mature into the "Queen of the Underworld." First, she is her mother's child. Her closest relationship is with mom, and not her father. Often the father has been absent during her growing up, or only home on occasion. Typically, a Persephone is an only child who remains an eternally youthful little girl.

There is a passive component to her personality that says, "Tell me who I should be." This is especially dominant during a Persephone woman's teenage years. During this period, she can be very insecure regarding her own self-worth and have a limited view of herself. Women who continue in the Persephone pattern tend to dress like little girls for a long, long time. Often they appear youthful looking. A Persephone woman's child-like openness and vulnerability make her charming. Her innocence, acceptance, and vulnerability are attractive—and empowering—to men.

Another side to Persephone is her ability to go into the subconscious realms. Dreams, imagery, and reveries are second nature to her, and she uses them with great skill. As she matures, she goes through the process of confronting her shadow self. As she faces her fears, she is a guide to others, helping them move through their dark side. She's been down there, she's been through it, so she can help others. Rather than being a little girl, Persephone becomes "Queen of the Underworld."

A negative Persephone gets stuck in "the little girl."
She doesn't know who she is. She is unaware of her own
desires and strengths, and remains uncommitted to a
relationship, a job, or anything. Nothing seems real to
her. It's as if she is waiting for Zeus to descend. "When is
my life going to begin?" is her plaintive cry. Because she
is trying to find someone who will accept her, she goes
in and out of relationships one after another. Persephone
women may go through some pretty brutal treatment
by men. They constantly attract males who devalue
them. Often, they are physically abused and emotionally bullied. What do they need to learn from that?
To value themselves!

THE PERSEPHONE SPIRIT

*Once upon a time, there was a princess, and the
princess was very sad. She had lost her golden ball.
A hideous toad hopped up to her and said he would find
her gold ball, but in exchange she must do two things
for him. They must eat dinner together that night, and
then she must go to bed with him.*

*So great was her desire to regain the golden ball,
the princess unhesitatingly agreed to his terms. In a
short while, the toad returned with the golden ball, and
that night, at dinner time, the toad returned again. They
dined together, and after the meal, the toad demanded
the other part of their agreement—that she go to bed
with him. But the princess refused. In a fit of indignation,
she grabbed the lecherous toad and threw him against
the wall with all her force. The toad became a
handsome prince.*

The Persephone woman is insecure, and usually
will submit to authority of any kind or take any kind of
male who comes along and remain in dysfunctional

relationships, subject to both verbal and physical abuse.

In the myth, the golden ball is a symbol of her true self, her wholeness, which gets lost. And the toad is the ugly part of her, or the situation or relationship to which she must learn to say "no" for transformation to occur! When she finally says no to the toad, she gets the prince. It may be literally a man, or the Prince may be symbolic of a newly-claimed part of herself that completes her.

Both Virginal And Vulnerable

Aphrodite—
Goddess Of Magnetism And Sexuality

INSTINCTUAL, MAGNETIC, SEDUCTIVE, SENSUAL, POWERFUL, FASCINATING, JOYOUS, MANIPULATIVE, BRUTAL, CREATIVE, PASSIONATE

Aphrodite is the awakener and the oldest of the goddesses. She gives life and renewal. She is the energy of pure sexuality. When an Aphrodite has union with a male, she can take him to great heights of rapture. Instinctive, magnetic, and sensual, she is moved by deep forces within her. Possessed of very sharp instincts, Aphrodite knows things at a gut level, and she is usually right. While some women are trying to emulate men, she wouldn't trade her femininity for the world! She loves beauty and she loves her body. An incurable romantic, she delights in being a matchmaker.

Negative Aphrodite can emasculate men, rendering them powerless. Once she has proved to herself that she can get him, the man she claims to love can be tossed aside. That's it, she's through with him. Men are very important to her, and she doesn't always care whose husband or boyfriend the object of her attention might be. The type of men who are attracted to Aphrodite are often macho bullies or beautiful and sensitive "maimed" young men who never fully grew up. Even if she has great talent, she may decide to give it up in order to marry some man not worthy of her at all. Union with a man can become a point of obsession with her and is often the dominant interest in her life.

THE SPIRIT OF APHRODITE

Once while lecturing on the goddess archetypes, I noticed a woman in the back of the room smile with recognition as I began talking about Aphrodite. As I described her attributes, she kept nodding her head and her smile broadened. "This lady does not look at all like an Aphrodite archetype," I thought. "Maybe I am being unclear."

Later during the conference, we had the chance to go to a public restaurant for our meals. And there I discovered how wrong I had been about her. Her body was out of proportion, short and shapeless—not at all the model for an Aphrodite. But she had a lively spirit and loved her body and, it was obvious, she knew how to make men feel good about themselves. The waiters couldn't pay enough attention to her. It was she who got "second glances" from men in the cloakroom and on the street. She drew the smiles from strangers constantly. She had "it"—the spirit of Aphrodite!

Goddesses Mirror Feminine Nature

In our search for identity and meaning, the goddesses can become our most supernatural allies. Take time to review these goddesses. Note which patterns and tendencies are most like yours. Which ones have the power or qualities which you need to claim your wholeness?

The following processes will help you invoke the aid of the goddesses.

Goddess Reverie

Within each of us there is a representative of the feminine spirit. This interior image is not necessarily one of the seven major archetypes, but is our ówn inner woman.

This experience is a way to contact her.

Start with some relaxing, meditative music playing softly in the background.

Lie down on the floor, or sit with your spine erect. Take a few deep breaths. Tune in to your body. Note where your tightness is, and where you are comfortable.

Focus on your face first. And then the areas behind your face. Breathe into your shoulders. Get a sense of releasing stress and tension. Notice where there is tightness in any part of your body. Speak to those parts. Tell them to let go.

Focus again on your breath. Connect with your breathing, slowly breathing in and out. Allow yourself to become warm, heavy. Continue breathing slowly and rhythmically.

Let the music carry you away from your reality. Walk across a great open plain. . . Feel the sense of motion as you walk. . . Breathe in the fresh air around you. . . Notice the clear sky overhead. . . and hear the distant sound of a lone bird. . . . The breeze is blowing gently across your skin.

In the distance, a great mound rises from the horizon. . . You feel drawn to this mountain, you are attracted to it. Begin to walk the path toward the base of the mountain. At the foot of the mountain, there is a spiral, winding path. Step on the path. . . .

As you climb up the path, notice the lush greenery.

Breathe in the pure, fresh mountain air. Sense the exhilaration as you climb higher and higher. . . .as you grow nearer and nearer to the summit. . . . .

Observe and walk...climb higher and higher. . . Now you are at the top of the mountain. Notice a cave there. Approach the entrance to the cave. . .Lower your head and enter. . . .

As you enter, you are greeted by a group of maiden girls, dressed in white. Notice how they greet you as they bring you into their midst. Hear their delicate voices as they sing. . . .

There is a knowing inside you that this is a time of preparation. You are being made ready to meet your own goddess.

One of the women gives you a white rose, and you are taken now to the edge of a pool of crystal clear water. . .You enter the water with the rose in your hand. The water is soothing, tepid. The water refreshes you, and you begin to swim effortlessly, gracefully. . . .

Now take a deep breath and dive beneath the surface. Be aware of the colors and the forms you see as you glide noiselessly beneath the water. . . .

Now you become aware of a strong light, and you are drawn toward it. From deep beneath the surface, feel yourself moving toward the surface until, with a great surge, you are free.

You are at the edge of the pool now. Be aware of the presence or form of who stands before you. Look at the ground and see her feet.

What shape are they? Notice her shoes. Is she wearing any? These are the feet of your goddess who waits for you. Now let your eyes move slowly up her body, observing clothing, texture, form, color. Move up the mid-section to the upper chest, the arms, the neck and finally, bring your focus to her face. Observe the features of her face. What feeling does she convey to you?

Spend some time with her. Stand together, or sit comfortably at the edge of the pool, or some restful place.

What is it like for you at this time to be a woman?

Your goddess has a gift for you. Receive it now, whatever it may be.

Bid her farewell. Step back into the water . . . swim with strength. You feel renewed, empowered. Feel what kind of woman you are . . . .

Step out of the water and move outside the cave . . . You start to descend the winding, spiral path, feeling that new sense of having made a profound connection to your interior woman.

Find yourself now at the base of the mountain. Walk across the great open plain . . . move back now to the room and start to bring the experience back with you . . . .

A Letter To My Goddess

In this exercise, simply address a letter to the goddess you wish to contact, and begin a communication with her. Ask questions, ask advice, share your thoughts and concerns, and listen for answers. This exercise is almost infallible for contacting your inner woman!

Norma came into the counseling session, bubbling with excitement. I had never seen her so joyful. She was wearing a stylish powder-blue dress with a bright pink scarf draped loosely around her neck. I could hardly believe this was Norma! A university professor, until now I had seen her only in conservative beige and brown pants suits. What a remarkable change!

With a broad smile, she reached into her handbag and pulled out her journal, and began playfully thumbing through the pages.

"I've been writing to Aphrodite," she said. Her

eyebrows arched up. "And I've been getting answers," she declared. "I asked Aphrodite what I should wear, and she said bright colors. I asked her if she wanted to go shopping with me, and she said yes. And she picked out this outfit!" Norma gave a bright sprinkle of a laugh that was a thorough delight. It was a pleasure to feel how much fun this was for her! She was a career-oriented woman with a background of high academic achievement. Now she was allowing herself to discover and experience a whole new dimension of her being!

She pointed to one letter after the next, describing little episodes and breakthroughs from Aphrodite. "For the first time in my life, I am really enjoying being a woman! And I love my body." And then her eyes filled with tears as she described a letter she had written to Hestia, asking for the wisdom of the feminine spirit.

"My brother and I have resolved our differences," she said. "I couldn't have done it without the help of the goddess."

Norma was discovering a new softness as a woman, and it was overflowing into many areas of her life.

Ritual For Evoking The Goddess Energy

Step One. Name The Name

Identify a situation in your life that is not working. Write it out in your journal, or describe it to a friend.

Step Two. Dismiss The False Power

Affirm that you no longer want this situation to dominate your life.

Step Three.
Replace False Power With Real Power.

Be still for a moment and acknowledge the Higher Power that is with you. Choose a particular goddess energy that you need to bring fresh energy and another perspective to the situation.

Visualize that particular goddess in action. What would she say? How would she act? What would her perspective be on the situation? How would she handle things?

Or, if you prefer:

In your journal, record the response that is given by the goddess.

* * *

As this process gets more familiar to you, when you are stuck in a situation, you can go through these steps quickly in your mind, visualizing the goddess in action.

* * *

Perhaps the biggest misconception
we have about love is that someone,
or something else, is supposed
to give it to us.

And so we dress to get it, decorate
our homes to get it, send our children
to certain schools to get it, join clubs
we don't like because we want it,
and choose professions and careers
that promise to achieve it for us.

We allow others to determine
how much love we get, when we get it,
how we get it, and what form
it will take—or whether we have
any love at all.

The one and only way to get
all the love we need is to find it
in ourselves. Self-love, the ability
to love ourselves, is our constant
quest—and at the same time,
our greatest challenge!
Without Self-Love there can be
no transformation.

CHAPTER 6

Self-Love Comes First

As I looked out over the audience, giving one of my first public lectures some ten years ago, I was surprised at how easy and natural it was. Two days before, Peter asked me, quite unexpectedly, to fill in for one of the speakers at a weekend workshop in Houston, Texas. The subject was "Dreams." The request to speak terrified me. I did everything I could to refuse. I just didn't feel ready or sufficiently prepared. I didn't have an outline. I hadn't any notes.

"Go ahead," Peter urged, "You're ready." I almost backed out. Now I was glad I hadn't. I was thoroughly enjoying the experience. My nervous tremor had evaporated, my jitters had dissolved, and I was feeling quite confident and capable, sitting on a tall stool, sharing experiences and processes for working with dreams to a very warm and receptive audience that filled the room.

The more I talked and shared, the more relaxed I became until, about a third of the way through the hour, Peter quietly slipped in and took a seat in the back of the room.

I was shocked.

What did I have to say about dreams—compared to him! Suddenly the words, the anecdotes, the information which had been flowing gracefully and effortlessly from me turned lifeless and leaden.

What was he thinking? Was he evaluating my performance? Every bit of self-confidence drained out of me, and every self-doubt I had ever known possessed me. I slumped into my seat and felt as if I were going to throw up. Whatever possessed me to think I was an authority on dreams! (Later that night, a friend told me I had turned visibly pale and shaken! In fact, she thought I had become ill.)

Suddenly, my agony ended in a flash. I was looking at myself from above the audience. I was literally floating out of my body, looking at myself on the stool from the ceiling at the back of the room.

And everything was different. The emotion, all the fear and confusion, was gone. It was a timeless moment of total peace. How differently the room and everyone in it looked and felt now! It was as though I had to lose myself to find myself. I was enveloped by love, and I could only see love and light in everyone else in the room. From there, Peter wasn't any more significant than any other person in the audience. He and I were equal, one and the same just like everyone else there.

There was a sense of deep peace: Don't judge, don't compare, and, whether you do well or not doesn't matter. You are loved anyway.

Then, just as abruptly, I was seated on the stool looking out over the audience again, without any fear whatsoever. All memory of what I had said just a moment ago was gone. I was totally disconnected from my train of thought. "If only someone would ask a question," I thought, "I could get right back on track. . ." Just then, a man in the front row raised his hand, almost as if he had heard my unspoken plea.

The whole experience happened in a twinkling of an eye, in a matter of moments—but it changed my life forever.

In that brief, intense, vivid, out-of-body experience,

my whole perspective of love changed. Up until then, I believed that love was something I had to earn by being good, by being beautiful, or intelligent, or dependable. Love was something that only came to people who worked hard to get it—and then they had to prove that they were worthy to keep it. Love only came in small packages, and there wasn't enough for everybody.

That moment was an experience with Grace. I didn't earn it. I didn't work for it. For some inexplicable reason, it was given to me. And from that moment on, I knew without a shadow of a doubt, love isn't something we have to earn. Love is something we discover—and we don't have to get "out of our bodies" to find it. It is present all the time, a vast ocean of energy that surrounds us. In the heart of our being, it's all that we are. It is our true self.

Our Biggest Challenge

To receive all the love, support, and nurturing we desire, we need only make one decision—and that decision is our hardest challenge.

We need to decide to love ourself, all of ourself, including our "uglies."

Exposing The "Uglies"

One of the special joys of my life was the year I spent working with the CETA program, helping women who were trying to get off welfare. I designed and taught programs that included self image, which was my specialty. Most of the women were black and uneducated. They had so little, but they had so much! Many were single parents and raising children on their own. They often didn't know where their next meal was coming from, but nevertheless, they had a natural joy and a willingness to laugh. As soon as they sensed that I cared for them, they opened their hearts. My fears of not being accepted because I was white, educated, and "privileged" quickly evaporated. They were soon bringing me pictures of their children. I knew I was "in." Invitations to weddings, shows, graduations, and funerals were extended throughout the year.

One day, Beatrice, a young black woman who was normally smiling and cheerful, came into my office and asked if she could talk with me.

"Sure, Beatrice," I responded. "What's on your mind?"

She sat in the chair next to my desk and slid her legs forward.

"Have you ever noticed I always wear slacks?"

I had noticed that she never wore a skirt, but hadn't thought about why. With a little reluctance, she explained.

"When I was growing up in Jamaica," she said, "I fell down and hurt my leg real bad. There weren't any doctors in my village, and the leg never did heal right." She pointed to her calf. "There's a hole here— it's my 'ugly.'

It's very ugly and I'm afraid if I show my legs, the other girls will laugh at me."

I was very touched by her self-conscious dilemma. At the time I was trying to cover up "uglies" myself. My life was full of confusion. My separation was only two weeks old and I was still struggling with hurt, pain, guilt, and all the other uncertainties that come with such a major upheaval. And yet to Beatrice, I looked like the paragon of authority and effectiveness.

"Beatrice," I said, "What would you say if I said to you, I've always wanted to wear skirts and shorts, but I am afraid others will laugh at me because I have this ugly hole in my leg?"

Beatrice shrugged her shoulders. "Hell, I would say you are crazy—wear them anyway!" Suddenly her face lit up when she realized what she had said, and she laughed loudly. How easy it is to accept and love other people's "uglies" and not your own!

"Beatrice, my uglies are not as obvious to you," I said next, and began to share some of what I was dealing with—and concealing—in my life. From that day on, in the classes, we began unlocking and sharing our secret "uglies." The trust and caring that poured out from everyone in the class was overwhelming.

We all have our "uglies" and to love ourselves we must accept them, whatever they are. Once we accept them, we won't need them to keep us from feeling loved. This experience is similar to the power we gained from being able to accept the Bitch or Bitches in ourselves.

Self-Love Makes The Difference

Rita was a woman who didn't know how to love herself. When I first met her, she impressed me as one of the most negative women I had ever known. She was convinced that she was a victim of life. She was working in a large government agency in Dallas. Her boss was terrible to her, the people around her were insensitive and uncaring. Absolutely nothing was working for her.

She came to me for counseling several times, and during one of the sessions I asked her to draw a "Family Portrait." This is a process similar to the "Parent Picture" described in the Dragon Fight chapter, except that instead of drawing the parents, all the family members are represented.

Rita drew two sisters exactly alike, and when I asked her about them, she said she was a twin. Then I asked her which was her sister and which was her. She looked at the paper blankly and said, "I'm not sure. I don't know which one I am."

Rita didn't know who she was! She didn't have an identity! "Am I my sister—or am I me?"

We worked on building her self-esteem, and finally she got to the place where she could say, "Hey, I've got my own separate identity. I'm not my twin. I'm me, and I count!"

Rita began to love herself.

During the course of the next six months, everything began to change for Rita. The next time I saw her, there had been significant changes. She had a new job. Her boss treated her well, and the people she worked with respected her. Now when she goes home, she is not so stressed out from the job. Her only complaint is that she has to learn how to stop feeling guilty because she's feeling so good!

Stop Punishing Yourself

Caroline was a somber, joyless, young woman. She was quite attractive, but she kept her natural beauty concealed under a dull, drab exterior. Caroline had been divorced for three years and was employed by an accounting firm for a position "nobody else wanted." Her job was dull, thankless, and non-creative. She didn't like her work, but she was the only one in the office who could do it—and so she did. She had lost interest in returning to college to complete her degree, and felt trapped in the job. Her belief was firm—life was supposed to be difficult.

As I listened to her life story during the workshop, I stopped her at one point and said, "You know what I really think you are doing—punishing yourself!"

"Oh," she gasped, and dropped her head. "You're right," she said, and then she began to sob.

Three years earlier, Caroline made a poor choice of a marriage partner. A few weeks before the ceremony, she realized that it was a mistake, but she was afraid to go back on a decision and reluctant to disappoint her family. Caroline went ahead with the marriage, and it was a disaster. He was a drug user and he abused her. With a lot of pain and sadness, she decided to get out of the marriage, but part of her still remained "stuck in the mistake," feeling guilty because the marriage hadn't worked out.

"I messed up. I really goofed," she confessed through her tears, "so I didn't believe that I was supposed to be happy."

"You can't be a victim unless you agree to it," I replied. We both knew, at some level, she had made that decision.

"If a lot of outer circumstances aren't working for you," I explained, "then there's some lack of self-love in your life. And those feelings of lack and limitation that get acted out for you in the world reflect deep and hidden subconscious patterns that say, 'I'm not worthwhile; I don't deserve to have things go well. . . .'"

Self-love is something we can all agree we need. But if it just stays an idea or vague wish, it has little power. So I urged Caroline to get specific. "In what ways will it make a difference to love yourself?" I asked. We sat down together, and I encouraged Caroline to write on a sheet of paper, "I love myself, therefore . . ." and to make a list of all the ways that loving herself would make a difference in her life.

On the sheet, she wrote:

I love myself, therefore . . . I am going to complete my college education.

I love myself, therefore . . . I will check into scholarship possibilities.

I love myself, therefore . . . I am going to choose a

career that I enjoy.

Two years later, I received a long letter from Caroline. It was from the Caribbean. Inside the envelope was a photo of Caroline in a scarlet bikini. She had become a marine biologist and was on a research expedition. The work was fascinating, the people interesting—and she was having the time of her life.

Self-Love—The Three-Step Formula

Step One. Decide To Love Yourself

Simply thinking about yourself won't change how you feel about yourself. Self-love isn't anything that you can try to get or earn. You won't get love by wishing you could have it. And it's not a matter of being "worthy."

You simply decide you are going to love yourself. And if it takes more than ten seconds to make that decision, you've taken too long!

Step Two. I Love Myself, Therefore...

Deciding to love yourself will make a difference in your life. Be clear about how. Make a list. Be specific.

Step Three. Always Approve Of You.

Avoid needless and destructive self-criticism. If you do something you feel is ineffective or that didn't work, avoid judgments and condemnation. Notice what doesn't work, and decide to do something different the next time. When you catch yourself disapproving of yourself, immediately replace the negative thoughts with approving ones.

An Emerged Woman's List Of Therefore's...

I Love Myself, Therefore...I accept myself
 just as I am.

I Love Myself, Therefore...I wear Christian Dior
 underwear.

I Love Myself, Therefore...I release the past.

I Love Myself, Therefore...I can eat a hot fudge
 sundae and not feel guilty.

I Love Myself, Therefore...I can choose not to eat
 a hot fudge sundae.

I Love Myself, Therefore...I love my body.

I Love Myself, Therefore...I take time to be still.

I Love Myself, Therefore...I approve of me.

I Love Myself, Therefore...I take risks.

I Love Myself, Therefore...I don't have to
 wait for him to change to get on with my life.

I Love Myself, Therefore...I get help
 when I need it.

I Love Myself, Therefore...I claim what I want
 from the Universe and I expect it to respond.

I Love Myself, Therefore...I expect others to love
 me, and I am surprised when they don't.

I Love Myself, Therefore...I let go of managing
 and controlling others.

Create Your Own Self-Love List

I Love Myself, Therefore...

I Love Myself, Therefore...

I Love Myself, Therefore...

I Love Myself, Therefore...

I Love Myself, Therefore...

I Love Myself, Therefore...

I Love Myself, Therefore...

I Love Myself, Therefore...

I Love Myself, Therefore . . .
I Love Myself, Therefore . . .
I Love Myself, Therefore . . .

Self-Love Evaluation: Taking Care Of You

Suppose that you were responsible for someone that you loved and admired, and that person was coming to stay with you for a week.

If you really loved that person you would see that their needs and wants were taken care of, that they were comfortable, and, to the best of your ability, that everything would work for them during their visit. In other words you would do everything you could to show you care and value that person.

If you would do that for another, why not for yourself?

Or as John Roger says, "Take care of yourself, and then take care of someone else."

Do it in that order!

Write out your answers to the questions below on a separate piece of paper.

How Do You Treat Yourself?

Take a few minutes and review the past week in your life. How did you treat yourself during this time? Go through the week day by day. Look for patterns, moods, self-talk. Would you recommend to a good friend that they live the way you have? Would you talk to or treat this friend the same way you treat or talk to yourself?

How Would You Treat An Honored Guest?

Take a few moments and think of some of the

people you most admire and appreciate (No limitation on who they can be—historical, political, mythological, or contemporary personality). Imagine that person is coming to visit with you for a week. How would you welcome her, what would you do for her, what would you do to make her feel comfortable, appreciated, valued? And then compare that with the way you treat yourself!

A Meditation On Self-Love

Close your eyes, and inhale slowly, filling your lungs with your breath. Now sigh it out. Relax and empty your mind, and let your thoughts float away until you find yourself in a lush green meadow.

Look around you. The day is warm. The sky is clear. The breeze blows refreshingly across your skin, your cheeks, and through your hair. Listen as the wind gently rustles the leaves. Hear the sound of a brook in the distance as it splashes and gurgles over moss-covered rocks.

Walk barefoot in the grass. Feel the coolness of the earth under your feet.

And now across the meadow, notice a form of someone coming toward you.

You watch the figure as it approaches closer. As it starts to come near, you are aware that this figure is you.

Now the other you stands in front of you.

For a moment you allow yourself to feel every feeling, think every thought you have ever had about yourself, all the things that you identify as you.

Look deeply into the eyes before you. Reach out and hold the hands of the form in front of you.

Be aware that there have been those times that you accused, blamed, criticized, and judged yourself.

Be aware that there have been those times that

you did not love yourself as much as you loved others.

Be aware that you did not always consider yourself worthy of love.

Be aware that there have been times when you have not treated yourself well.

Now start to reach out and enfold this other being, all the parts of yourself. Allow yourself to send all of your love and caring to this self. Decide at this moment to totally accept this you. Acknowledge that you are all right just as you are and say to yourself:

I am forgiven.

I feel forgiven.

I am not promising that I won't make mistakes in the future.

I am not promising to be perfect and happy. I give myself permission to be imperfect and happy.

I give myself permission to enjoy being me, even when I fail.

Now say:

I love, (say your name).

I am who I am, and I love me.

Now stand in the meadow and let all those good and warm, beautiful feelings about yourself fill you up, and give thanks for this experience. And now be aware that an overshadowing Presence fills the meadow. And this Presence is Love, a vast cosmic infinite sea of limitless energy that permeates everything above, below, around, and within you, extending as far as your imagination can take you.

For a few moments, allow yourself to be immersed in that Presence, fully and unconditionally.

And then, when you feel ready, open your eyes, and bring all that awareness, all that love and caring back with you.

Among the ancient Greeks
there were three names for Love:
Eros, Philos, and Agape.

Eros is a dependent-based love:
"I need you and I love you."

Philos is a security-based love:
"It's safe and I love you."

Agape is the highest form of love.
It is a love that is extended
unconditionally and given by choice:
"I see you and I love you."

CHAPTER 7

Three Kinds Of Love

Snappy Whitside, otherwise known as Warren Webster Whitside III, took a liking to me. And I hated him for it.

It happened one day in the third grade. Snappy came in late, apologized to Miss Earl, the teacher, and headed directly to my desk. With a great flair that seemed to capture everyone's attention, he ceremoniously placed a carefully wrapped package on my desktop, smiled proudly, and backed away.

"What was that!" I fretted. It wasn't my birthday. It wasn't Valentine's Day or Christmas. And Snappy wasn't my boyfriend! Alan Hammock was! Alan was a year older and in the fourth grade. It was obvious we were in love. At least, it was obvious we were boyfriend and girlfriend. We exchanged notes and flirted with each other during Wednesday afternoon choir practice. Occasionally, Alan even held my hand. And, at least once, we had played "spin the bottle."

I stared at the present on the desk and scowled. The audacity of Snappy Whitside giving me a present—especially in front of the whole class. Maybe it was a mistake. Maybe he didn't mean it for me at all. I wished it would go away. It didn't. So I decided to ignore it. The first hour passed. The bell rang, and it was time for math. The package sat untouched on my desk. We were well into our lesson when Snappy raised his hand in exasperation.

"Teacher," he said, "I saved my allowance for three whole weeks to have enough money to buy Betty a present, and she hasn't even opened it."

Oh no! I couldn't believe it! It wasn't a mistake. He did really mean it for me. I could feel my cheeks burn, and I wanted to squeeze myself into a ball and disappear.

Miss Earl was a rigid and precise teacher. Somehow, though, she always had a twinkle in her eye. I hoped she would stop this nonsense and silence Snappy. Instead she seemed quite delighted.

"Well, Snappy, that's very nice of you," she said. Then she smiled and looked over the whole class.

"Oh, no, she wouldn't," I groaned, sinking deeper into my seat. But she did.

"Class, let's gather round Betty's desk and see what Snappy's bought her." The entire class crowded around my desk, with Miss Earl and Snappy the closest to me. I was angry, embarrassed, and humiliated. It was a horrendous feeling. I was the center of attention and there was no choice but to open the package. In order to shorten the ordeal, I unwrapped it as quickly as possible.

It was a bottle of perfume!

Some of the girls giggled, raising their hands to cover their mouths. One of the boys groaned, and another gave Snappy a teasing little push. Miss Earl thought it was probably the cutest thing she had ever seen.

While my classmates giggled and groaned, I put the bottle down and seethed.

"Betty," Miss Earl said, "why don't you say 'thank you' to Snappy."

"Thank you," I managed to hiss through clenched teeth, barely above a whisper.

At recess, Snappy, who was very aware of my

irritation, came up to me on the playground and said, "Betty, you may think that you hate me. Just remember this, the line between love and hate is very thin."

What! I was furious all over again! It wasn't possible that love and hate were almost the same. It couldn't be. I loved Alan and I hated Snappy. And those feelings weren't at all the same!

The thought stayed with me for the rest of the morning. It went back and forth in my mind. At the lunch hour, I raced home, still wrestling with this question. I wanted an answer. I needed to know. What is the difference between love and hate! I banged through the front door and ran into the kitchen. Mother had the table set and was waiting for me.

"Slow down," she shouted as I raced through the house, and there was no more conversation until I could settle down.

It seemed like an eternity, but after a glass of milk and a bowl of soup, I asked the day's burning question.

"Mother, Snappy Whitside says that the line between love and hate is very thin. What did he mean?"

Mother looked at me from across the table.

"Betty, would you like some more chicken noodle soup?" she replied.

I guess she didn't hear me.

It took me a long time to discover that the opposite of love isn't hate, it's indifference. It takes a certain amount of caring even to bother hating someone. Hate is simply misdirected love. I guess Snappy was way ahead of me.

My quest to understand what love is began with Snappy Whitside. Over the years, the challenges, the opportunities, and experiences along the way have taught me a great deal of what love is and what it is not. And this I know:

We want to love.

We want to be loved.
We may not always know how to love or be loved.
So we settle for a lot less than what we could have.

Three Kinds Of Love

Eros: "I need you and I love you"

"Falling in love" • magnetism • passion • intensity • projections • fantasies • matching weaknesses • control • possessiveness • enmeshment • co-dependency • seeking approval outside self • emotional • playing out the Dragon Fight with your partner • working through "your stuff"

When we are babies in our mother's arms, her arms belong to us, not to her. To the infant, the mother is nothing more than an organ, an extension of its own body. That is our experience in the womb, and during the first year or two of life, we require, demand, and expect our mother to respond automatically to all our needs, just as if they were her own—our fears, our discomfort, our anger, our hurt.

As the infant grows, it fights to maintain control of what it considers to be its own. It uses many forms to maintain control—crying, anger, physical strength. All of this is a determined effort to get its mother to behave as an extension of itself.

Our first relationship is one of unity with another. Then as our experience grows, separation results. Very early, we realize the inevitable. "I am me, you are you, and our needs are different." Undoubtedly, our needs as individuals will, at some point, clash. And each of us, being most interested in self-preservation and in obtaining what we want, will find it necessary to work harder to fill our needs, even at the expense of the other person's. And then, out of a need to protect and defend ourselves, we will create what is known as an ego barrier. At this point, we will take on independence, personality, assertiveness, and even aggressiveness.

The urge to know ourself as a separate individual continues as we grow into adolescence. At this age, we have become aware of ourselves as distinct units, separate and apart from our parents. We recognize we have rights of our own, including the right of self-expression. In most cases, the ego barrier is very well established by this age. The "tough guy," the "Mr. Cool," the sarcastic, upbeat, young girl you see walking down the halls of every junior high school in America are all expressions of this very precisely designed tool, created for handling life's experiences as well as interactions with others.

Ego barriers are not honest. They don't reflect our true selves. Instead, they express an image that we believe will attract people to us, or will cause people to admire us and want to be like us, assuming that will assure acceptance by others. We have developed a set of "games" which are not genuine, but which serve our purposes to a degree.

And then Eros strikes. Eros, the "blindfolded god," shoots us with his arrow—and that arrow crashes right through all the ego barriers and protective devices that we have so carefully built—and we "fall in love."

It occurs dramatically, suddenly—which is why we refer to it as a fall. It is seldom, if ever, a choice. It happens to us, like falling off a cliff. In almost all of its occurrences, we are victims of the experience. Eros relationships happen at random, generally with a person of the opposite sex, but especially without regard to reason or logic. They often don't appear to make sense.

Eros relationships are very physical, very emotional. Eros love works through the hormones, the glands, and the organs, affecting the emotions in erratic ways. It manipulates auric fields, electricity, and magnetism, sometimes resulting in feelings, thoughts, and actions heretofore unheard of. We call this experience "love," when in fact, it has nothing to do with love in the sense of true love, or Agape.

Typically, at this stage, we don't really "fall in love" with the person—but rather with who we want that person to be. Eros love tends to be very unrealistic. We project and fantasize qualities and expectations about our partner. We project our own repressed maleness (or, in the case of a man, his femaleness) on to another, and we "love" that person because we think they have something we don't have. We believe that they hold a quality which we are unable to express, and so we want them because they have what we need. We reach the point of saying, "I need you, therefore I love you."

Then at some point, the inevitable occurs. We begin to realize that those imagined qualities really aren't there, never were. We begin to see the partner as he or she really is, no longer just as we want him or her to be. The love potion wears off, and the experience becomes painful. Why? Because it hurts to "fall out of love."

We can't accept them just as they are, so we don't see them as they are. We don't accept or see them clearly because we can't do that for ourselves. We don't see ourselves as acceptable. We are not whole yet, so we are looking for someone else to complete us by filling in the missing pieces. In Eros relationships, we attract partners who have what we lack. And when we find the missing piece, we think it's a match!

Almost everyone believes that falling in love is the basis for marriage—but falling in love is almost never done sensibly. Regardless of the fairy tales or the Hollywood promotions, falling in love with the right person is infinitely rarer than falling in love with the wrong person.

People fall in love because of matching vulnerabilities and insecurities, not because of matching strengths.

Eros is extremely powerful. The ego barriers that we have maintained so effectively come crashing down, and we "fall in love" in spite of not wanting or intending to! We are absolutely powerless. We can't help it. We are victims of Eros! And like Psyche on the mountaintop, we are swept away, albeit briefly, to a paradise with a lover whose face we are forbidden to see. And for a time, we have the experience of what it feels like to have a crashed ego barrier between ourselves and another. Defenses are dropped while we are enamored of each other.

This kind of falling in love, the intensity of Eros, is always temporary. It is the same experience that occurred in infancy with our mother acted out again—and the results are the same. There comes a time when the honeymoon is over. The questions begin as we painfully start to recognize qualities in our partner that are not exactly what we thought they were. The defenses are re-erected as the two lovers gradually begin to learn again that they are two separate people with separate identities.

Or, sometimes, we find someone else to fall in love with—because that's what most believe is supposed to happen. We cherish the ideal of falling in love and living happily every after. So we create our ego barriers one after another as we search for the "perfect" relationship. Most often, the two ego barriers are still damaged from past experiences when a new relationship begins, and a lot of "dirty laundry," unhappiness, misery, projection, accusation, guilt, and blame are carried into it.

Even in the best of relationships, there usually comes a time when we feel attracted to someone other than our partner. It is a rare person to whom that doesn't happen! And yet, we subject ourselves to a tremendous amount of guilt when it does! We begin to criticize ourselves. If I am attracted to another, that must mean there's something wrong with the relationship, something wrong with me, or wrong with my partner.

But it's simply not true. It means there is a match—a different type of match than the one that drew us to our partner, and that it has awakened new and different parts of ourselves. But it doesn't mean that we are powerless in the face of the attraction. Nor does it mean that we should leave one relationship to begin a new commitment.

Michael...

When I was working with cancer patients, I had many encounters that were both challenging and rewarding. The very nature of the illness and the time consideration requires people to open up very quickly.

I had a special connection with Michael, an attractive musician who was courageously fighting his disease. I found him sensitive, creative, and intelligent. As his therapist and counselor, I saw a lot of Michael, and he shared much of himself with me. He was a true romantic, and he sparked something in me which I had never felt in my marriage.

One day when I entered his room, there was a noticeable change in his attitude. Normally confident and open in his interactions with me, today he was nervous and insecure.

"Can I ask you a question?" he asked.

"Sure, ask me anything," I responded, not expecting anything out of the ordinary.

He paused for a moment, and then looked directly into my eyes. "I want to make love with you," he said. It startled me.

At first I felt an impulse to be annoyed, just as I had when Snappy Whitside gave me the perfume bottle. I wanted to put up a cool and distancing wall of professionalism. After all, I was his counselor. But the truth was that I was attracted to him as well. I had never voiced it—or hardly even admitted it to myself. Whenever these feelings came up, I dismissed them. Now, I was challenged. My option was to be detached and clinical, or to be honest and just be me.

With a deep breath to gather my strength, I smiled at him and said, "Michael, you caught me a little off guard. It's true, I feel very close to you, and you're attractive to me in every way. And I admit I have wondered what it would be like to make love with you."

It was very helpful to communicate in a very honest and open way, without roles or pretense. In my decision to be honest, a very real moment was created that linked our hearts.

"But, there's another part of me that knows making love with you would change our relationship. I'm married, as you know, and you have a special person in your life. It would change everything if we made love."

We talked for several hours. I realized that with him, I experienced feelings that were lying dormant within me. I was trying too hard to be a responsible wife and mother. I had no time for romance or whimsy, and Michael brought all these feelings to the surface. It was a lovely and exciting way to feel. But the love I felt for him—and the feelings he had for me—didn't need to be expressed in a sexual way. We realized that by caring for each other, by sharing from our hearts, and by being open, we were making love all the time—but in a different way. We made a conscious choice to deal with our feelings. The passion was diffused by talking about it, and it didn't have to be discussed again.

When Eros Strikes...Fear Not

Every woman needs to understand that whenever an Eros attraction comes along, even if she is already in a committed relationship, it's important not to be terrified. Remember, you have a lot of choices.

One choice is to deny your feelings because it doesn't happen to fit into the box or barrier that you've built for yourself. It's not what's supposed to happen when you are in a relationship! So you pretend it doesn't. When we deny these feelings altogether, they usually surface in a somewhat less direct way. Our behavior will be different around this person—and others will notice it, even if we pretend it isn't there, or we might become disgruntled with our present partner for no apparent reason.

Or you can choose to feel guilty about your feelings. Guilt is something we create in order to avoid making a decision to deal directly with the issue. A difficulty with Eros love is that we have been programmed to think that feeling and caring deeply about a member of the opposite sex means that we have to express those feelings in a physical, intimate way. Intimacy is such a rare feeling, that when we touch it, we don't know what to do with it—except go to bed!

Anytime a relationship is expressed in a sexual way, the nature of the relationship automatically changes. That is not to say that it is better or worse, but it does change things. Sometimes we are unwilling to take responsibility for our actions and we protest that things "just happened." It is a convenient response, and it is not honest. It is important that we be clear about the consequence of our involvements, discuss openly why we want that intimacy, what our expectations are, and what it means to us before entering any involvement.

And there are always other options. You can deal with the attraction by questioning the kind of energy you are putting out, exploring what is the connection between you and the other person. What part of yourself becomes alive around that person? Make a decision to develop that part of yourself without depending on someone else to stimulate those feelings. Understand the dynamics of the attractions and investigate the possibility of just being friends. These attractions provide us with new opportunities to self-explore!

Philos: "It Is Safe And I Love You"

Commitment to marriage • material goals • social pressures • sensible, reasonable, predictable • boredom • resignation • "what you settle for" • passive-aggressive • correct answers rather than truth • dreams of what could have been • strangers living in a strange house • quiet desperation • secure • stable home • supportive • appreciative • pseudo-intimacy

After the initial chaos of the Eros attraction, a relationship that moves forward and takes on commitment can settle into a monotone and go on automatic pilot. Instead of separation, divorce, or clandestine affairs, the two partners begin to settle for a relationship that is safe, secure—and predictable. This defines their love as Philos.

Philos means that we've been through the honeymoon stage, and now it's time to get sensible again. We've "fallen out of love," and we have begun to recognize ourselves as separate individuals again. At this point, the choice is to maintain a semblance of "marriage," acknowledging one another's values, while living reasonably together forever after.

Philos love is the kind of love that a man has for a car, or his career, or for anything that he has an interest in, but doesn't identify with to the extent that it crashes through his ego barriers. The Philos lover knows himself to be separate from the thing he loves.

The emphasis in a Philos relationship is usually material. The focus is on the next car, the bigger house, the better job, the nicer clubs—the values associated with the American Dream. Maintaining a lifestyle which is organized around a norm of what is considered to be proper and acceptable entails certain pressures and acceptance—from family, church, society, and peers.

And in an effort to maintain that lifestyle, often the deeper parts of self are suppressed or denied. Our deepest feelings and thoughts are sacrificed. Issues are dealt with but at a superficial level. "Let's keep it nice, fluff the pillows, and pretend that everything's all right." Often there is underlying passive-aggressive behavior while attempting to mechanically go through the motions. There is usually a genuine appreciation and respect for one another, though not a deep knowing of one another. Too often the partners now exist as strangers sharing common space.

There is sometimes a feeling of resignation, resentment, and boredom in Philos relationships. You talk, but you never talk, you look at each other, but you don't see each other. You can often observe Philos at work in restaurants where a couple faces each other across a table, having little or no conversation, simply eating their meal together, passing time. And perhaps the woman is thinking,

It could have been different...

If only he were different...

If only I hadn't given up my career...

If only we hadn't had children so soon...

The dream of "what could have been" continues in the back of her mind, accompanied by feelings of bitterness or blame toward her partner for not being the man she thought he was when they first married.

What is lacking in the relationship is usually not an unwillingness to change or open up, but rather a lack of knowing how to do it. So what is settled for is a lot less than what could be.

Sometimes the reasons for staying in the relationship are need-based. We need to keep the approval of family, community, church, *etc.* Even though the relationship may be unfulfilling, it might seem better than being alone. It may not be the best, but it is better than nothing!

On the other hand, a Philos relationship can be experienced differently. The commitment to stay in the relationship can come from strength. There can be a fierce determination to make the best of things, to keep the family unit together, and to provide a secure and stable home environment.

Once that commitment is made, there is no need to concentrate on what is "wrong" with the other person, but only a decision to make positive change within self. In that way, we learn to take full responsibility for our own happiness, not burdening someone else with it, and we know that our decision to stay with the partner was a choice. There is always power in choosing.

Agape: "I See You And I Love You"

Love by choice, rather than happenstance • lowering the ego barriers gently • kindness • giving up selfish interests • openness • truth of past and present • empowering each other • common ideals • shared vision extending beyond the couple • supporting spiritual growth • understanding • complete trust • intimacy (on the aesthetic, emotional, physical, and spiritual level) • unconditional love

Agape is not something that "happens" to us. It is choosing to love, a decision we make in response to a person, people, or a situation. It is not the phenomenon of falling in love that we find in Eros. Nor is it resignation to a situation believed to be unsatisfactory yet unchangeable, as with Philos. Agape is unconditional love, the rarest form of loving.

Agape is beautifully expressed in the Biblical story of Ruth, when she says to her widowed and homeless mother-in-law, "Whither thou goest, so shall I, Your god shall be my god."

We find it again in the love of David and Jonathan. Both men were willing to defy their king (and Jonathan's father) for the love and protection of one another. Agape echoes in the poetry of Sappho who wrote passionate verses of her friendship for the girls in her school. We see Agape between sisters who share and give of themselves to one another. It is shown in the devotion of a mother for her child, and in the animal who gives up its life for its master.

It is acted out when someone gives up self-interest for the sake of the beloved. It is extending self for others.

Extending ourselves means that we are willing to do things that are not necessarily in our own personal best interest. It means caring and doing more than is required, not because we have to, but because we choose to, even when it is inconvenient. An important point to note: in Agape love the giving is not experienced as sacrifice but rather is a willing choice from the heart. That level of loving can only come when the giver knows and loves himself so is not giving to get love back.

For couples, Agape love holds the image of two whole people standing side by side, sharing a common ideal. The love then expands and can reach out to many.

In my experience, one couple stands out as a perfect expression of an Agape love relationship. For many years, the woman raised a family while her husband served as a career officer in the armed forces of his country. When he retired, she began her career as a doctor. He has retired from the military and now helps organize her busy teaching and traveling schedule. Both of them work as a team helping people together. Their love is not exclusive, yet their relationship is unique. The two have become one through a common ideal and purpose.

When we lift ourselves to the experience of Agape love with another person, we are able to share life in oneness. "Two become one" doesn't mean that we build a fence around ourselves to keep others out. Rather, we create a cooperative and mutually supportive venture in expressing and exploring boundless love.

Exercise For Identifying Kinds Of Love

Reflect for a moment on three important relationships of any kind, past or current, that are, or were important in your life.

Assess the kind of love that exists in each relationship. Was it need-based, security-based, or unconditional? A combination of one or more?

Most of us are convinced
that we want love and marriage, secure,
enduring relationships, kindness,
support, empathy, and understanding.
We hope for these things,
and attract partners and relationships
that give us less—even the opposite
of what we seek.

The unconscious mind contains
"hidden agendas"—unrecognized,
unintegrated, unknown parts of the self.
Until these hidden agendas are
recognized and resolved, we'll stay stuck
in one or more of four kinds
of relationship patterns.

CHAPTER 8

Co-Dependency And Other Hidden Agendas

I remember, as a child, lying awake at night with thoughts of what my life would be. These thoughts were more than fantasies of a youngster exploring what she wanted to be when she grew up. Instead, they were communications, clear directions from within, that my purpose was to do a spiritual work and that I would travel all over the world, teaching and sharing. As I closed my eyes, I was shown faces of people I would meet many years later and places I would eventually visit. This panorama of things to come, this *deja vu*, would cause my heart to race, and sleep would be impossible. In a deliberate effort to calm myself, I would concentrate on something more easily understandable, a treasured line in a favorite poem, the antics at a friend's Birthday party, or something interesting that had happened that day at school, and eventually I would lapse into sleep.

I "knew" as well that someday there would be a male partner with a similar vision. And there was a feeling of what that relationship would be like. I envisioned two people standing side by side, lovingly joined in a common goal, reaching out to others. Perhaps, this is the "future memory" Patricia Sun refers to. We all know innately what a true-love relationship is, and there is a genuine yearning to experience that. Yet, often what we observe in the relationships of others and what we experience in our own lives falls short of that ideal. What we don't always know is that in order to achieve a whole, lasting relationship with others, we must first perfect the relationship we have with ourself.

We Get What We Want

In relationships, we receive exactly what we want, not necessarily what we ask for.

No one enters a relationship saying, "I really want to be punished because I am unworthy of being truly loved, or, "I'm really looking for a partner who is going to belittle and ignore me because, down deep inside, I feel that's all I deserve." We are convinced that we want loving relationships: commitment, marriage, integrity, companionship, friendship, affection, warmth, kindness, support, and understanding. That is our conscious mind speaking. We hope for these things and attract partners and relationships that give us less, and even the opposite of what we seek. Why?

The dichotomy occurs because there is a split between the conscious mind and the unconscious mind. The unconscious mind has our hidden agendas, the unrecognized, unintegrated, unknown parts of the self. Until they are resolved, they determine the kinds of relationships we have.

Once we become honest with ourselves and are willing to identify and transform these parts of self that don't serve us, then what we want and what we ask for become the same. We can consciously *choose* and *expect* loving relationships in our lives, and we can have them.

Christy Got Exactly What She Wanted

Christy was a thirty-nine-year-old therapist who came for counseling. She was pretty, except her face was clouded with sadness and etched with worry lines. Christy talked in low halting tones about her first marriage, an unhappy union of six years. She had been young, she explained defensively, and had hoped for more with her second marriage. It started out as all that she had envisioned. But it became impossible and it dissolved like the first. "Soon after we were married, he became someone else," she said with a sigh as her face dropped again and she began wringing her hands.

She felt now she was clear about her priorities: love, marriage, and a family. And she was very specific this time about the qualities she wanted in a man: someone attentive and interesting, someone intelligent, and, in order to satisfy her maternal urges, this person must come with a ready-made family.

"I'm getting too old to have children of my own," she explained. And so the list continued. Christy had actually written all these traits on a "shopping list"—and the very next day that intelligent, attentive, interesting man with a ready-made family appeared in her life.

"Imagine, my surprise," she said. "I couldn't believe it. He was interested in me, and almost from the start, he began talking about marriage."

They had been dating for six months when Christy came for help. This "perfect man" had all the external requirements Christy had listed. In addition, he had just been offered a top post with the government, owned two homes, and was fluent in seven languages. He was extremely attentive—when he was with her, that is. But there were long periods when she didn't hear from him at all. At other times, he would promise to call the next day and would "forget."

After Christy explained the background, she got to the crux of the matter. Mr. Perfect had recently been hospitalized, and when she visited him, he told her he wasn't sure anymore about their relationship.

"He needs time to think," she sighed, dropping her head and wringing her handkerchief into hard, tight knots.

"What else did he say?" I asked, sensing there was more to come.

"He said that, although he had had difficulty with his marriages, he was glad that his friend thought enough to send him flowers." Christy looked up, eyes brimming with tears. "I didn't even know he had been married more than once! Is this the man for me or not?"

Christy got what she asked for, an interesting man, educated, intelligent. And she also got what she wanted, an uncertain relationship, stressful, insecure, repeating familiar patterns that were programmed in childhood. When she was a child, her father left home. Her memories of him are clouded, unclear, uncertain. Christy still "wants" this vagueness. Though it is not comfortable, at least it is familiar. As an adult, she is vague about who men are and uncertain about interactions between men and women. This syndrome is typical in women, when they did not know their fathers or when their fathers were not available for them, except intermittently or sporadically.

Though there are aspects in Christy's present relationship that are rewarding, overall it is not supportive and fulfilling. He does not call her when he says he will, there are unanswered questions about his past, unaccountable time lapses between their meetings, while at the same time he poses interest in marriage. As long as Christy has not resolved her early childhood patterns and believes that this is the way she should be treated, she will continue to draw men that will re-create uncertainty. Christy is emotionally co-dependent.

The Hidden Agendas: Co-Dependency In Relationships

Co-dependency is a term that was originally used to describe the disease affecting the wife, children, and others closely involved with an alcoholic or drug-dependent person. Those persons were seen as being co-dependent on that addiction. In other words, it became apparent that the "helpers" and caretakers to the addicted person had heavy psychological and emotional investments in that addiction. Each person had his or her own cluster of addicted traits.

The term "co-dependent" has now become so expanded as to include a wide variety of behaviors. In fact, some therapists assert, in desperation, "Co-dependency is anything—and everyone is co-dependent." For example, the workaholic represents a form of co-dependency. In the office this person is likely to burn out, sacrificing himself for the job. They are the caretakers for the incompetent. They make excuses for a demeaning boss or place an inordinate value on their position. But underneath there is self-neglect.

Co-dependency is always an elusive search for self-esteem. According to Ann Wilson Schaef in her book, *CO-DEPENDENCY: Misunderstood, Mistreated*, the perfect co-dependent ". . . is someone who gets her identity completely from outside herself. With little or no self-esteem or self worth, she is isolated from her feelings and spends much of her time trying to figure out what others want so she can give it to them."

With this definition in mind, it is possible to see how an underlying dependency on others for self-esteem

can be a subtle but powerful force, not just in relationships that have a substance-abuse factor, but in any
relationship that is not healthy.

In the case of Christy, she is still emotionally
co-dependent on anxiety, suffering, and suspense. She
wouldn't put herself in this painful situation if there were
not a part of her that wants it. She expects the upheaval,
the excitement, the drama that goes along with it. The
man definitely carries the stick in this relationship, while
she remains addicted to the emotional turmoil provided.

To end her co-dependent pattern, Christy has to
resolve unfinished issues with her parents, enhance self-
esteem, and develop healthy ways of interacting with
men. A beginning step would be to experience men as
people first, men second and to eliminate her requirements for relationships to "be" something and just allow
men to be. As she cultivates male friendships and she
learns to be comfortable with men in a natural and
spontaneous way, she can discover not only what men
are like, but how it feels to be around men who are
supportive, open, and honest.

Co-Dependency In Relationships

Co-dependency is the elusive search for
self-esteem.

Co-dependency is the underlying foundation
of Eros love.

Co-dependency exists when either one or both
partners look to the other to fulfill the needs they have
not yet fulfilled within themselves.

Co-dependency exists in any of four areas: Mental,
Emotional, Material, and Spiritual.

Unhooking from relationship co-dependencies
can be every bit as difficult as getting unhooked from

chemical dependency. The addiction and pain of withdrawal can be just as severe.

Mental Co-Dependency

Mental co-dependency exists when we want or need someone to make decisions for us, or consider someone else's ability to make right choices superior to ours. Or we may depend upon a man to make our decisions, not because he is superior, but simply because he is a man, especially in choices concerning children, finances, politics, and lifestyle.

My marriage exemplified mental co-dependency. When I met Sean, he was several years older than I, experienced, and mature. While Sean was responsible and warm, he often suppressed his feelings and was, as well, controlling. I played the Pleasing Passive role, agreeable, compliant, never making waves. While I was happy and fulfilled in my role as mother and content with the amenities provided by the relationship, I surrendered my connection to a deeply felt sense of spirit and to the intuitive knowing that I could and would accomplish more. I opted for comfort and security and became dependent on Sean for material needs, as well as for major decisions concerning family, lifestyle, and finances. I sustained the dependency by sitting on my opinions as well as my feelings.

It took some time to realize that I had allowed myself to become dependent on someone else to make my decisions. I took even longer to understand that I had chosen to give my power away to my partner and to others.

Emotional Co-Dependency

Emotional co-dependency is present

whenever we look to others to create our emotional excitement or to provide for our emotional stability. There is an innate drive to re-create the same emotional patterns that we experienced with our mothers and fathers. They feel familiar. There's a certain security in their existence even if they are negative patterns, such as anger, aggression, uncertainties, emotional highs and lows, demeaning and belittling attitudes, being kept off guard, upheaval, unsatisfied longings, emotional distancing, punishment, sarcasm, rejection, and pain. In fact, the more dysfunctional our earlier patterns were, the more insistent we are in repeating them. We will attract partners who are capable of re-creating the same dramas for us. The little girl in us is saying, "Fix me up, I am hurting."

Often there is a sexual element in an emotional co-dependency. We might depend upon a compelling sexual energy to keep the excitement alive in a relationship that may not be supportive in other areas.

Joan is a good example of how an emotional dependency evolves. Her parent's lives were too busy and complicated, and, in essence, they gave Joan to her aunt and uncle to raise. She was split between two families and not always sure that her parents loved her. When she married, she chose a man who was overbearing, macho, and a womanizer, a man who gave little affection or emotional support.

Joan's husband was critical of her cooking, her weight, her looks, her clothes, and on and on. She felt insecure and unsure, just as she had with her parents. Her biggest fear was that he would leave her, and he did—through his escapades with other women. On occasion, he was physically abusive. Finally, in desperation, she left the marriage and immediately became infatuated with a married man. It was a passionate love affair with the drama of clandestine meetings and secret phone calls. There was the anxiety of not knowing where she stood with him or whether or not the relationship would last. The anxiety, fear, and loneliness are familiar replays of early patterns. She's been accustomed to them from childhood. The drama, the upheavals, even the pain, she equates with love. She will continue drawing these difficult, even impossible relationships into her life until she establishes another model of what love is and becomes clear about what she deserves and what she wants.

Material Co-Dependency

Material co-dependency is present when a woman feels that she cannot earn a living on her own, or feels trapped in her relationship that provides for her material security. She may want to maintain a certain lifestyle or status as "Mrs. Somebody"; at the same time, she resents her dependency on "Mr. Somebody." The dependence on materiality is a definite love substitute.

Harriet was born into a poor family. She described her father as an argumentative, accusing, blaming alcoholic. Her mother was strict and critical, often focusing on what she didn't do rather than what she did accomplish.

As a child, Harriet witnessed her father having incestuous relationships with her sisters. She both hated him for it and simultaneously craved his affection. She experienced her mother as a strict authoritarian with unbending rules and regulations. Neither parent gave her the emotional support she needed. She felt denied.

Harriet doesn't want to be like her father or her mother, so she strives to be the opposite. She became very successful in her career, highly respected, and financially secure. However, like her father, she doesn't give attention to her children. Her father escaped through alcoholism; she escapes through her work. And like her mother, she's distant and emotionally non-supportive to her children. Deprived of emotional support and attention, her children give her serious problems. Unlike her parents, though, she has the means to buy their love and gives it as a love substitute. alcoholism; she escapes through her work. And like her mother, she's distant and emotionally non-supportive with her children. Deprived of emotional support and attention, her children give her serious problems. Unlike her parents though, she has the means to buy their love and gives it as a love substitute.

Harriet doesn't realize that the men she attracts into her life are very much like her father. Both her father and the men in her life are emotionally immature. The only difference between her father and these men is that rather than being under-achievers, they are over-achievers. Not ever feeling really loved by her father, she is never sure that these men love her either. They may lavish presents and gifts on her, but she never gets what she really wants—the gift of real feelings. Because she hasn't experienced real love, she finds herself emotionally dependent upon a love substitute—money.

To resolve this situation, Harriet needs to develop the power of the feminine within herself and to know its strength: feelings, compassion, touching, affection, nurturing, risking, and being vulnerable. As she opens to her gentleness, she'll automatically attract a partner who will reflect her loving capacity, not just one who simply fulfills a need for image and material gain.

Spiritual Co-Dependency

Spiritual co-dependency is the need for someone else to inspire or enlighten us. When we assume that someone else is closer to God or more spiritually aware than we are, we look to gurus, guides, "channels," and "god-women" or "god-men" to provide answers. We look to them to direct us, and are more willing to listen to their spiritual truths than to follow the truth in our own hearts. This is not to devalue the role of a true teacher, but the relationship with any teacher must be scrutinized.

Coleen was born into one of America's wealthiest families. At the age of three, she was forced to make an excruciatingly difficult choice. Her parents were separating, and she was asked to choose which parent she wanted to go with, without being told which ones her brother and sister had chosen. Coleen chose her mother, and her brother and sister went to live with their father. Years went by before Coleen ever saw the other half of her family again.

Coleen's father was a rigid, left-brained businessman who lacked the ability to express feeling and affection. He was aloof, matter of fact, and proud. Her mother was an alcoholic, self-centered, non-feeling, erratic, and unable to provide positive guidelines to her daughter. Though there was material abundance, Coleen received very little nurturing as a child.

As a result, Coleen felt insecure, had fears about expressing herself and showing affection, and carried the guilt and burden of the divided family. Underneath she wondered if she was really worth loving. To protect herself, she became a loner who felt safer with animals than she did with people. She knew that she could trust her horses, and she could also trust her money. Her security became money and horses.

As an adult, male relationships are mostly nonexistent for Coleen, with the exception of two important men, both spiritual teachers. She doesn't trust monied men, because her father deserted her, and she finds poor men unappealing. Powerful spiritual teachers—the men who are one step beyond what money can buy—attract her. Her heroes are men with a mission, and they don't require an emotional involvement on a personal level, which she's not equipped to deal with anyway. This way, she has the father figure who was not there for her earlier, and she's able to avoid interacting with a man on an intimate or personal level.

Coleen's main challenge was to validate herself and know that she didn't have to use money to buy love. She needed to learn to value her genuine sensitivity and caring, how to share herself more freely with others. As she began opening up more to her true self, she took the "god-man" off his pedestal. She realized the power is not in him, but within her.

More Hidden Agendas

Unrecognized hidden dragons come back to haunt us.

Sandra was an attractive woman who continually had relationships that were either impossible or unfulfilling. Her father had been sexually abusive, and she grew up resenting him and feeling unloved. Her problems with partners, she felt, resulted from that painful childhood experience. When love did not come her way, fears would creep in and she would give in to beliefs that she was unlovable and doubts that she would ever have a supportive partner.

Although her problems certainly seemed to lie with the father, when she explored the issues more deeply, she eventually realized that her deepest resentment was with her mother. Not once had her mother stepped in to save her and protect her. As a result, whenever Sandra was treated unkindly by individuals, the "mother" part of herself would not step in to alleviate her doubts and fears, and the pattern kept repeating. As she began to recognize and understand the pattern, she stopped allowing negativity to control her. When she observed herself thinking negative thoughts, she learned to replace them with positive ones instead. She took responsibility for loving herself in a way her mother had not been able to do. As she began to express more care and kindness toward herself, other people began to treat her with the same consideration.

We Never Resolve Anything When We Move To Its Opposite. Attracting A Mate Who Is The Opposite Of Our Problem Parent Does Not Resolve Our Real Issue.

If your mate is the same or opposite to your problem parent, it probably indicates your issues with your parents have not been resolved. They are just disguised or ignored. Resolution only comes when we no longer need to be the same as or different from our parents, and when we no longer need our mates to be the same as or different from our parents. We allow instead our parents to be who they are, and we make our choices in relationships from a space of confidence. When we are dealing with the same or opposite, we are still reacting. True choice only comes when we respond, rather than react.

Leona was the child of a passive father who, without warning, would occasionally go into a rage and become overpowering and abusive. The mother, on the other hand, denied her feelings and refused to express them. Leona married young. Her unconscious decision was, "I don't want to marry somebody like Dad." And she didn't. She married a man much like her mother: mental, non-feeling, distant, aloof. Much to her surprise, instead of remaining the passive, shy person she was normally, she began repeating her father's pattern of explosive anger with her husband. She became like her father while her husband played the role of her mother.

The marriage ended, and she began looking at herself. She used visualization to heal the relationship with her father. She diffused her Shrieking War Goddess by expressing her feelings when they came up, even if it was uncomfortable. She matured in her capacity to speak out, to express, and to share. After several years without a significant male relationship and with many inner changes, the relationship she attracted was much more balanced, reflecting her newly-developed identity.

Overvaluing Or Undervaluing Our Mate Means We Are Still Caught In The Saint-Sinner Game That Began With Our Parents.

As long as we think one parent was superior to the other, there will be an imbalance within our masculine and feminine selves, and this imbalance will be reflected in our relationships.

When one parent is over-glorified while the other is undervalued, we are not looking at either parent for what they are: real people, equal in value, both having positive and negative qualities. We are stuck in the saint-sinner syndrome; and we will either overvalue or under-value our mates. This affects our relationship to our self as well. When a realistic view of the parents is accomplished, when the gold as well as the challenges they provided are appreciated, then our masculine and feminine aspects come into harmony.

Jeanette's mother was strong, capable, and responsible. Her father, on the other hand, was ineffective and needy. Although he made an adequate income, he came home to bury himself in the television and expected his wife to take care of him and make all the decisions concerning the family. He didn't want to be involved. There was very little communication or expression of caring.

As the oldest child, Jeanette felt overburdened with responsibility. She developed beliefs that men are weak and ineffective, not to be counted on, and that life is hard. She married a passive-aggressive man. They clashed from the beginning. Re-enacting the mother, she became demanding and righteous. Not knowing how to deal with her, her husband shut down, repeating the role of her father. The marriage ended after five years. Then, Jeanette threw herself into her work where there was a safe place to express her strength. She had a series of relationships that were not supportive. The men she attracted were like her father. They wanted to be mothered. She both nurtured them and resisted that role, switching into the Castrating Female and the Mother Superior.

As Jeanette began to explore her patterns, she made a conscious effort to come to balance within herself. One of the first steps was to take her father out of the negative role. She eventually found a balance between her own gentleness and strength, her own responsible and nurturing sides. The result was that she attracted a more integrated partner.

Anna's mother lived for her husband in a self-sacrificing manner. She lacked a good sense of her own identity and tended to be non-communicative and passive-aggressive. Anna's father was a highly successful professional man with wide interests and sophisticated tastes, a lover of the arts, music, and culture. He offered Anna positive values and clear guidance, though he was controlling and rigid at times.

For Anna, the parent on the pedestal was her

father. She, like him, became a high achiever and chose a profession he encouraged. Even in appearance, there is the attempt to be male-like. Since she values men more than women, her friendships are almost exclusively with men. Her significant other relationship is a carbon copy of her father. Her partner is an older, refined, successful, professional man, who is strongly opinionated, dominating, and somewhat inflexible.

Although Anna is highly successful as an attorney, she is still looking for guidance and approval from a strong male. She views her mother as weak and ineffective, and unconsciously wants to be the opposite of her, although she repeats her pattern of dependence on the dominant male. Anna undervalues the female part of herself: the emotions, the feelings, the ability to nurture. When Anna opens to this part of herself, acknowledging that gentleness can be strength as well, she will no longer re-create her childhood pattern. Also, she will uncover, initiate, and sustain female friends.

Every Person That We Attract In Our Life Mirrors Some Part Of Ourself, Even If It Is Not Obvious What That Match Is.

When somebody does something that really bothers us, our negative reaction is because we either do too much or too little of the same thing. In other words, what we react to most in other people is that part of ourself that we haven't owned or acknowledged. It may be exaggerated or underplayed in the other person, but it mirrors a similar or opposite pattern of what we do. Otherwise, we wouldn't react. For example, when writing this book, I was helped by a friend who is a sensitive and creative writer. One day he called to say that he had lost a couple of pages from the manuscript. What! "Lost" a couple of pages. How could he? This astounded me. It was mind-boggling! Now, I would have to remember what I wrote and try to re-create those two pages. So I went back to my type-writer, muttering, "How in the world could he lose a couple of pages?"—and I couldn't find the pages that I had just been working on! That's an exact mirror, a perfect match. Instead of judging him for being scat-tered, I could see in him that part in me that needs to get better organized. At the same time, his creativity and mine match as well.

Exercise For Looking At Co-Dependency

Take another look at the same three relationships you used for the previous exercise. Consider whether these relationships reflect one or more of the four kinds of co-dependencies. Do you recognize the same pat-terns of codependent behavior in all three relationships, or are your codependent patterns different in each rela-tionship? How do any patterns you may recognize relate to patterns of behavior with or between your parents?

The purpose of all relationships
is to become conscious and to awaken love.
Being conscious means taking
responsibility for what we are creating.
We all have partnerships of various
kinds in many areas of our lives.
That is a given.
The choice is only
who we want to learn with,
and whether we want to avoid, deny,
or prolong the time it takes for us to learn.
This chapter gives real-life,
practical examples of how to assess
the main partnerships in our lives,
and understand our role in attracting them.

Partners We Attract And Why

"Who should I be today?" I would ask my older brother, John, as we played our favorite game. "Should I be 'Betty' or 'David'?"

And John would decide my identity for the game.

It never occurred to me that I could make the choice for myself. John was my best friend, and we were as close as a brother and sister could be. We were growing up in the Ozzie and Harriet era of the 1950s, in Front Royal, a small, conservative town nestled in the Blue Ridge Mountains of Virginia. Women were passive, destined to be wives and mothers, and men made all the important decisions in life.

If John said, "Be Betty," I would let my long, blonde hair flow freely, put on a pretty dress and shiny black patent leather shoes. We played store, school, or church, or I would dutifully clean up my room and practice the piano. Betty was always pretty, pleasing, and agreeable.

On the days when John said, "Be David," I would get a glint in my eye, and I would run into my room, braid my hair, put on jeans and sneakers, and off we'd go, running, climbing, laughing and rough-housing, exploring jungles, fighting battles, and creating adventure.

It was exciting to be David. He was bold, assertive, and competitive. My idea of being feminine was confined to the limited cultural models of the 1950s and Front Royal. It is not surprising that I depended upon John, the significant male peer in my life, to give me the permission I needed to express the freer part of my nature.

For years I continued to require men to tell me who I could be at any given moment—"Betty" or "David." I became what my boyfriends, husband, bosses, and teachers expected of me. I had no idea that there was another option. As "Betty," many times I felt victimized, betrayed, and angry that the adventuresome, fun-loving, outgoing me was being squelched. And "David" could make me feel scared, alone, and abandoned. I was afraid of claiming my own power and making my own decisions. It took me many years before I realized that it wasn't a matter of being either "David" or "Betty." I could merge both parts of myself, the male and the female together, and become a whole woman, I could be both gentle and strong.

Our Patterns Are Learned Early

Our ideas about who we are and how we behave with others are learned early. We chose those patterns. We also choose how long we want to stay in them. The purpose of all relationships is to become conscious and to awaken love. Consciousness means taking responsibility for what we create. It also means that when we notice that what we are doing is not serving us or realize we are going back into old patterns, we change. And we change quickly, not waiting sixty years, or six years, or six months, but moving closer to six minutes or even six seconds. Knowing, all the while, that since we create our pattern, we can transform them. We can be who we want to be.

The real nature of woman is love. We want to be able to give love and to be open to receive love. All relationships are an opportunity to practice being who we really are.

No matter what life situations we have chosen for ourselves, we will nevertheless interact with many relationships, many partners of various kinds in our lives.

Usually the term partnership implies the meaning of the significant other in our life. Some of us have chosen one committed relationship. Others have experienced a series of relationships with bits and pieces that have been learned with each encounter. And some of us are not in any significant other relationship. There are many reasons for that: we are scared, we are in the process of healing, we have chosen not to be for a variety of reasons, real and unreal, or we don't know why.

I am extending the term partnership to include not just significant others but also those who are in our inner circle. They are partners of another kind: children, bosses, teachers, friends, business partners, *etc.* Beyond this circle there is our outer circle that includes everything from the grocery checker, whom we see occasionally, to every other person on the planet, with whom we share a partnership simply by nature that we live on the same earth and are committed to either destroying or bringing life to one another.

Which is to say we can't avoid learning, so if we are in a committed relationship most of our learning about love will probably be in that partnership. If we are not in a committed partnership it just means that life will present our lessons in more clever ways. The sales clerk is quite capable of presenting us the perfect opportunity to mirror part of ourselves.

Our choice is not whether we have partnerships. That is a given. The choice is only who we want to learn with and whether we want to avoid, deny, or prolong the time that it takes for us to learn.

The most important relationship we will ever have is the one with self. All other relationships mirror that one. The kinds of relationships we have, therefore, are totally up to us. The only person that ever has to change to make a relationship different is us. As we change, those around us automatically reflect that change. They will tell us in their response to us what we really believe about ourselves and who we are inside.

It is imperative for every woman who is interested in transformation to examine honestly the partnerships that she has attracted. It is usually the ones in the inner circle where the most growth comes.

Be willing to look at:

- The positive qualities that attracted you to that person (probably what you have in yourself as well as what you wish you had)
- The negative qualities (your disowned parts)
- The response to this person that didn't work (for example: The Shrieking War Goddess)
- Co-dependency, if any (not that it was emotional co-dependency, but the specific emotional co-dependency, for example: uncertainty)
- The gold: what was the value from the relationship? What did you learn—the positive change?

My Personal Purpose

From earliest childhood, I had always carried a strong inner knowledge that my purpose in life was to do a spiritual work. This feeling of a "calling" began about the age of four and stayed until my last years in college. I can't remember a time when I wasn't intrigued with things of the spirit, the mysteries of the inner life. The part of me that was called to do a spiritual work I called "Elizabeth." And there was "Mary"—the part of me that was intrigued with the mystical, the inner world of dreams and intuition. These were hidden parts of myself which few people knew, so almost everybody called me "Betty."

In college, I wrote away to several seminaries. I thought both my work and my purpose in life could be fulfilled by a life in the ministry. But the responses were disappointing. All their programs seemed too confined, too rigid, limiting, and too constricting. There seemed no place to explore what I was looking for, no place where I could study the things that fascinated me the most. Near the end of my college years, I began to lose my faith in the dream, and I began to listen to "Betty," that side of myself that had been taught by many voices that "Life isn't like that. Be reasonable, get practical. Get your head out of the clouds. Stop being a dreamer!"

No special partner appeared with a shared vision. And then I met Sean, the man who became my husband. Sean didn't know about the "Mary" me or about "Elizabeth." He married "Betty," and Sean and Betty had everything that society considers the ideal—the perfect marriage. Sean was the prominent attorney, Betty was his attractive, competent, educated wife. We had a big home on the river, lots of status and plenty of money. We had everything but a common goal and a shared ideal. And a relationship without that will always be a limited one. For seventeen years, I concerned myself with form, appearance, and role, constantly trying to live up to what others expected me to be. Betty opted for comfort and security, and in exchange surrendered her connection to that deeply-felt sense of spirit and to that intuitive knowing that her life was to be one of purpose and service. In Betty's life there was little room for Mary, and no work for Elizabeth. They withdrew to a deep place within me, and I lost their address.

Eventually my marriage came to an end. At the time, I thought it was because Sean and I did not share the same ideal, and I wanted to grow. There was no room to breathe, and an underlying restlessness that was somehow not being dealt with. I didn't know then that it was possible to make changes within myself and within the marriage. It seemed divorce was the only option.

Positive Qualities	Challenging Qualities	Response

Similar background
Responsible
Family man
Financial security
Warm
Secure
	Philosophical
	  differences
	Suppressed
	  feelings
	Control
		Pleasing
		Passive

Co-Dependency	Gold

Mental
(Making major
  family decisions
  and choices about
  life-style)
Material (financial
  security)
	*Motherhood
	*Find own identity
	  and change the
	  direction of
	  my life
	*Stability

And with the divorce came that painful, awesome, confusing, challenging experience of being a woman in transition. A woman in transition is almost always unclear and uncertain. She is no longer the person she used to be—and she doesn't know yet who she is. If the relationship ends because the man leaves her, she is angry. If she ends the relationship, she feels guilty. In transition, the woman is dealing with the beliefs, patterns, and expectations of the past. It is a time when a woman will swing from one extreme to another—from being prim and proper perhaps, to being reckless and adventurous. She often makes rash, impulsive choices with painful results. At the same time, the transitional phase can be a period of risk-taking, fun, and experimentation. Most of all, it is a time of self-discovery. My transition was all of those things.

Relationships which begin during a time of transition seldom last. When a woman is in transition, she isn't whole and attracts men who mirror her own incompleteness. The relationships tend to be "fast burners", repeat performances, or reactionary. The "fast burners" are intense, with a lot of fire, but short-lived. The repeat performance is a duplicate of what was just left. It's the old stuff all over again only with new names and new places. There may be the sudden realization and the wanting a quick exit, the resignation and the determination to somehow make it different this time, or the most painful dilemma—you just don't see it. Then there are the reactionary relationships when you get the opposite of what you just came out of, which means you're still dealing with the same issue.

During my transitional period, three male figures became significant, each mirroring different aspects of myself. Two of the men were already friends, but with the change in my life, they took on different roles. We are drawn to those experiences that can help us wake up out of our illusions and teach us about love. And relationships are often our greatest teachers because we are forced to see ourselves through others.

It is not surprising that after my safe, secure, and predictable marriage dissolved into divorce, the next phase of my life would be a startling contrast to everything I had known before. At some level, I knew I needed a crash course in opening up—and that's what I got.

Opening The Heart—Jason

Jason was delightful, charming, fun-loving,

generous, imaginative, wise, creative, and above all, magical. Jason was constantly celebrating the simple joy and the great blessing of being alive in a universe filled with the most incredible and delightful surprises, like seashells and fairytales, rainbows and music. With Jason, time always seemed suspended. I might not see him for months and then we would spend a couple of days together and it would seem that months or years of adventure, excitement, magic, and incredible peace were compressed into those brief hours. He indeed was a mystic, a man with a rich and deep inner nature. With Jason, I learned the language of dreams, the world of symbols and subtle energies. It was through him that dreams became my best friends. I looked to them for guidance, accepted their wisdom, and trusted them completely. He had a profound understanding of the dream world, and I had an aptitude and an eagerness to learn. Also Jason encouraged me to develop inner disciplines: to practice yoga, to appreciate solitude, and to listen from within. To Jason, people were sounds and scents, and I began to see and hear with his sensitivity. Above all else, Jason had an open heart. His greatest gift to me was his ability to make me feel loved, valued, and appreciated as a woman.

The relationship encompassed a nine-year period. We were dear friends, sometimes brother and sister, or sometimes teacher and student, and eventually we became lovers. In many ways we were cut out of the same cloth. There was always a special grace surrounding our union as though there was some kind of divine dispensation. Often, magical things seemed to happen when we were together. I began to understand the phenomenon of "synchronicity." If we decided we wanted some apple pie, at the next corner there would be a sign, "Today's Special—Apple Pie!" If we ventured into the woods, a mist would suddenly appear, making the setting more charmed. I would be teaching in California and circumstances would bring Jason to the same place at the same time. The pieces on the giant chess board definitely moved in our favor.

Jason was quick to help me with difficult decisions and ready to help me see another perspective. He was the knight who did battle for me. (Later, I recognized aspects of mental and spiritual co-dependency). If I ever needed him, I would simply think of him and within twenty-four hours there would be a welcome, "Mary, what's on your mind?" Somehow it seemed our relationship was not limited by time or space. At some other level we were deeply, perhaps eternally, connected.

Then it began to unravel. Seeing Jason only periodically over the years limited our relationship. How lofty and lovely things can be when meetings are only intermittent and in unfamiliar and exotic settings. But when it is time to spend extended time together, the inevitable occurs.

We had gone away to the Outer Banks of North Carolina to design some workshops together. As long as we focused on our work, things went well and the creativity kept flowing. But when things switched to the personal level, I felt a dominance and over-control from Jason. From his perspective, he was simply trying to help me get through some "stuff." By now, I was weary of the teacher role. It wasn't what I wanted or needed. Jason and I had played the "I'm higher, you're lower" game too long, with Jason the teacher and me the favorite student. However, no games can be continued unless, at some level, both agree to keep playing.

Every relationship requires a graceful shift in roles, sometimes brother-sister, mother-child, father-daughter, teacher-student. But if we get stuck in one role, it makes a real friendship and partnership impossible. There was another issue, though, that went much deeper and that I couldn't see until much later. I was still in La-La Land, not wanting to risk and commit totally to any one thing or any one partner. Jason had been patient and infinitely resourceful in presenting relationship possibilities, but the time for patience was over. He was definitely a knight on a quest, but his quest would take him in a different direction.

The return trip was bittersweet, an ominous prelude for the inevitable finale. Whereas before, we had always sensed a sphere of protection and love surrounding us, now it had somehow vanished, leaving a noticeable vacuum. Everything was off. To begin with, when we left the hotel, we missed the ferry. While we waited for the next one, we took a walk on a desolate beach strewn with dead fish. On the road back to Virginia Beach, a German Shepherd leapt out from the bushes. Jason swerved to avoid the dog, but not in time. The Shepherd was stunned and ran off limping and whining into the woods. We searched for her and even went to the local store to try to identify the owner, but to no avail. What made this episode so potent was that twice before a German Shepherd had saved Jason's life. It was clear. The magic had left us. We were not able to move the relationship to the next level. After nine years, the relationship had run its course. It was over and it was painful.

Several years later, I had a lucid dream. In my dream, a friend from Holland was telling me her dream. As she recounted the dream, I began interpreting it for her. The interpretation flowed clearly and effortlessly, as if Jason were speaking through me. It was exactly the kind of clarity I had seen him demonstrate many times. Now I was experiencing it myself.

At our last meeting, Jason had said I no longer needed him. Now I could see it was true. Through his sensitivity and depth, he had given me a powerful gift.

With this dream, I knew how powerful that gift was. The transfer was complete. Some relationships are not forever. They are given for a particular time and a special purpose. He had been my guide, my bridge from one world to another. But there comes a time when you must walk on your own. I no longer needed Jason to reflect the Mary that was awake.

Positive Qualities	Challenging Qualities	Response
Creative Sensitive Generous Intuitive Optimistic Supportive Open hearted Wise	Secrecy Higher/lower games Loner	Pleasing Passive

Co-Dependency	Gold

Mental (clarity)
Spiritual (wisdom)
	*Love and
	   appreciate life
	*Heightened
	   sensitivity
	*Value self
	   as a woman
	*Depth/intuition

No Turning Back—Peter

The urgency in my brother's voice first prodded me to meet Peter. James and I had spent several years together studying and discussing the Source material channeled by the great American clairvoyant, Edgar Cayce, and James was convinced that Peter Davidson was as gifted a psychic as Cayce.

At that time, I was sure my "guru" stage was over. I had already made a pilgrimage to India to explore the wisdom of the East. There I met a spiritual teacher and we began a correspondence that lasted for two years. I felt I had outgrown the need for that relationship, and wasn't looking for another outer "teacher" to guide my inner growth. So, with some reluctance, I agreed to meet James at the center in Virginia Beach where Peter conducted his Sunday service. I had just parked the car several blocks from the center, and was pulling the keys out of the ignition, when I noticed a man walking down the street. He was dressed in a frumpy brown polyester suit and wore a matching gold tie and shirt. I had a strong prejudice against polyester. Not only that, it seemed a tasteless combination. His salt-and-pepper hair was slicked back in a way I found unappealing. He was clean shaven, though in a few weeks he would grow the beard that later became a trademark. His physical appearance in no way attracted me; yet he seemed very familiar. But from where and from when? I flashed back to my childhood deja vu. I suddenly recalled his face from a sea of many I had seen on the screen during that flash into the future I had experienced as a child. I somehow knew him already. There was a vitality about this stranger, a certain enthusiasm as he walked, a sense that he walked with God. "That must be Peter," I thought. Even at a distance I felt power radiating from him, and sensed an inner connection to him.
A power surged through my body like an electrical current, from the crown of my head to the tip of my toes. I sat in the car for some time, wondering if I should go into that service. If I did, I somehow knew my life would never be the same. My premonition proved correct.

Peter conducted a communion service that day, and the blessing he gave was, "Expect to be changed by this experience." And I was! There was no turning back. Elizabeth, the woman with a purpose, had been awakened.

There was something so alive in Peter's words, so clear in his teachings that a slumbering, dormant part of me responded vibrantly to his vision. And I felt a spiritual depth, a return to my real self. My association with Peter lasted twelve years. During that time, he was mentor, beloved friend, and brother—and the most outrageous, paradoxical, and unpredictable human I have ever known.

Almost from the start, Peter encouraged me to teach. Often, I taught with him in a variety of settings: London, New York, California, Texas, Israel. Other times, I was off teaching by myself. Being with him sparked my creativity and challenged my mind and capacities to the utmost. I loved being pushed to the edge.

One of my first experiences with Peter has been one of my most treasured. My brother James and I were visiting Peter, chatting in his living room when there was a loud insistent banging at the door. In bounded a disheveled man of about forty, smelling of alcohol and somewhat shaky, badly in need of a shave, wearing rumpled clothes that looked like they had been slept in for a few days. The man was obviously in a lot of pain. He wasn't familiar to any of us, but he had been to one of Peter's services several months before. He had been touched, and in this time of crisis he was reaching out to be heard, to be helped. Peter stopped everything and just listened intently. The man was incoherent at times, but the compassionate attentiveness of Peter and his few well-chosen words quieted his troubled spirit and gave him the reassurance he needed.

What struck me even more was the look on Peter's face after the man left. It was ancient, yet timeless, a look of total compassion and heartfelt love. It was one that I was to see often during the years we were together.

With Peter, I had many experiences with Higher Mind and altered states. Peter opened the door to new dimensions of reality for me. One time, early in our relationship, Peter and I were at a conference in Chicago. Harmon Bro, a popular lecturer and writer on the Edgar Cayce readings and a personal favorite of mine, was on the program. That evening Harmon was recalling the arrival of his fourth child. He was in the waiting room at the hospital all alone when he started to hear music. But there was no audible sound, no piped-in music. He realized that what he was hearing was the music of the spheres, the sounds that accompany the birth of every soul. I felt as though my heart had been pierced. Tears streamed down my face.

The next evening Peter was the featured speaker, and after his talk, I experienced what Harmon had described. Peter finished his talk with a healing service. With the audience singing Alleluia as an accompanying sound, Peter invited anyone who wanted healing to come up for the laying on of hands, I felt the urge to go forward, and when Peter touched my forehead, it felt as though the top of my head opened and there was an enormous funnel rising up through the heavens. I went into another reality. I was still aware of the faint Alleluias in the background, yet I could hear ethereal music and see indescribable colors of other dimensions.

This "opening up" was one of many experiences with altered states that I had with Peter, but there is a very subtle danger in a relationship with a "god-man." One needs to always make a clear distinction between the experience and the catalyst. Once that distinction becomes blurred, there is an unhealthy transference and there can be the dependence upon someone else for the source of your spiritual experience. It can keep you from developing and trusting your own inner source.

On the personal level, there were different challenges and paradoxes to be resolved. On the one hand, the experience with Peter and his spiritual organization was rewarding and fulfilling. There were opportunities to teach, learn, and share in a common goal with a dedicated group. The impact was far reaching, extending even into Europe, Africa, and Australia. I thrived on the broad scope of the vision. And it was rewarding to see people's lives being changed. I was kept so busy with the newness of it all, with the travel, teaching, planning, organizing, contacting people—all of which I found so stimulating—that the Dragon Fight almost escaped my notice.

Unresolved elements of my father-mother Dragon Fight were being played out with Peter, and for much of the time, I was an unconscious participant in the battles. The same qualities I had admired in my father were transferred to Peter. There was an admiration for his knowledge, a yearning for his philosophic understanding, a respect for his authority and strength, and an absolute delight in his humor. The deep feelings I had so naturally and openly felt for my father were transferred to this other wise, strong man. And the same uncanny attunement to my father, the knowing of words before they were said, the sensing of feelings, even if they weren't expressed, was also a parallel. Both men were my beloved "rabbis."

As with my father, I respected Peter's authority, and reacted against his control. I was special to my father and to Peter. Part of me enjoyed the specialness, and I played it as the Pleasing Passive and Rescue Me Maiden, remaining in the background in a support role, devoted to Peter and his work.

But as time went on, I noticed that, with my over concern for Peter's welfare, his health, schedule, and organizational needs, I was losing a sense of my own boundaries (the neglect of self is typical of the co-dependent). I became alerted. Underneath the passivity and niceness, there was hostility. The anger wasn't directed at Peter, but at myself for being emotionally, mentally, and spiritually co-dependent. Of course, the anger was veiled, just as I had disguised the anger I sometimes felt toward my father as a child.

Peter was very much the center of his organization, with the rest of the staff playing a supportive role to his leadership. As my work started to expand, it became more difficult for me to keep a balance between supporting Peter and attending to my own needs. My relationship with Peter shifted. Now, instead of the Priceless Madonna, I began feeling quite the opposite.

"I want you by my side, but you aren't committed to the work. You only want to do your own thing!" he would say.

And I would seesaw, afraid to be on my own, yet wanting to be on my own. As my work developed, I could see it was going in a different direction than Peter's and I couldn't see how the two could merge. If I were going to be a partner as he suggested, I needed to make a full-time commitment to his work. And though I resonated with much of Peter's vision, there was another stirring in me that could not be quieted. Peter could not understand, nor embrace that stirring, and I would not and could not deny it.

We both vacillated. He was as inconsistent as I. Peter made it clear that he was married to his work. Any relationship beyond the scope of that work was a distraction. On the other hand, there were periods when a strong personal relationship developed, with wonderful moments of tantalizing closeness and intimacy. There was too much fear, and not enough trust. I wanted to pull away; I didn't want to pull away. I felt torn. "I want you by my side, I want you as a partner." And then, "A personal relationship interferes with work." He was a perfect mirror for my own indecision. A friend, yes. A teaching partner, yes. A personal partnership, no. It was never a real consideration. In fleeting moments it had crossed my mind, but I would quite readily dismiss the thought as too oblique, not real. The confusion was a fierce loyalty that went beyond anything personal. That wasn't so easily dismissed.

It took me a long time to accept the truth. I wanted out, but I wasn't honest enough, or clear enough to choose it. For two years, I had a strong sense I had learned what I needed. It was time to go. When we ignore the inner promptings, out of fear and insecurity, we pay a price. Instead of letting go and following my heart's desire, I began questioning and criticizing every-thing about Peter, his lifestyle, and his organization. It was time for me to move in a new direction, but instead of simply choosing to go, I blamed and found fault. The continual changes, which at some subconscious level had previously seemed fascinating, and which on the mental level I had the rationale to explain, now seemed like a vortex of confusion. I had moved from one side of the pendulum to the other. And nothing is ever resolved when we seek the opposite.

One particular day, I was spending some time with a good friend. I was feeling moody and irritable. The mood deepened and my friend tried to help turn it around. As we talked, something was triggered that was embedded deep inside, an anger, a rage that had been there from childhood—and I turned it on him and became so angry I thought I could have killed him. Lucky for me I was with a gifted counselor. When he recognized what was happening, he shifted to a centered, supportive stance. He may have been the target for my rage, but he recognized it wasn't him I was mad at.

"Look, you can trust me," he said. "Whatever feelings you want to express, whatever you need to say, this is the time to do it. Go for it!"

That was all the permission I needed. I felt safe and supported. Suddenly, all the dark feelings and emotions I had politely suppressed and denied for so long came pouring out like an uncontrollable torrent. I wailed and sobbed, I grieved and stormed and mercilessly flailed at my pillows. I was encouraged to go further.

At first, it was an anger at Peter, and then at my former husband, and finally diffused anger. Then, from the depths of my self, from the very core of my being, a rage and resentment surfaced toward my father. Buried memories and forgotten feelings bubbled up. I recalled the times when he let me down, when he didn't stand up for me, and when he denied me the special time I needed. The heartache and the tears seemed endless. I felt helpless and overwhelmed, as though I had tapped into an unending sea of pain. My fear was that I would be trapped, a prisoner with no way out. I reached a moment of deep catharsis. The timing for such a moment can never be planned. Though it can be assisted, it must occur somewhat spontaneously. I knew I could not be forced into my depths, or I would feel the pressure to perform. I had been given the sacred space to be totally one with the experience, to allow it to happen, neither forcing it nor preventing it. There was a subtle moment when I knew that I could stuff it down again as I had in the past, or go with the experience. I decided to go for it. There was a deep release. I felt an overwhelming sense of love. In that moment, there was no more need to punch the pillow or wail and scream. A sense of freedom and peace enveloped me. My father no longer had to be the flawless, faultless paragon of strength and wisdom. He was a human being, with faults and virtues. Now, I could really love him. The final remnants of the Dragon Fight were over at last and it was time to say a final farewell to the Pleasing Passive.

The catharsis resolved the paradox with Peter. The issue was no longer whether I was for or against Peter and his work. The focus shifted. I was ready to follow my own heart, listen to my own rhythm, and move into a different phase of my life's work and purpose. There was no confusion, no conflict, nothing to fight for or against. It was a natural process, not to be feared or denied, but welcomed and embraced.

Two dreams validated this new direction. In both, I was sitting at a table, face to face with Peter, talking directly and clearly. Peter's beard, which I associated with his public image, was missing—a symbol of being able to see him clearly, as he really was. The masks were off and the fantasies were over. We communicated with openness and directness, with no longer the need to adulate or unfairly criticize. He was a beautiful man, a gifted teacher. From these dreams, I realized I had come into balance with my male side. I had the courage now to follow my own inner authority. The paradox had been resolved. I was at peace.

Positive Qualities	Challenging Qualities	Response
Determination Inspiration Awareness Faith Compassion Knowledge	Feeling overvalued/ undervalued Unpredictable emotional swings Shut off feelings	Pleasing Passive Wilting Bitch

Co-Dependency	Gold
Spiritual (knowledge) Emotional (upheaval and uncertainty)	*Get my own inspiration *Take responsibility for own work *Empowered to teach *Knowledge

Coming to Clarity—Francis

In my myth, Peter was the powerful king, and Jason was my shining knight. The king is a man of authority, of truth and understanding. The knight goes in quest of the high ideal, is romantic and magical, there to fight battles for me and be my protector. Both the knight and the king enjoyed a fair lady at their side. With both, I played the "Pleasing Passive" all too frequently.

Jason opened my heart, and Peter connected me with Higher Mind, I was definitely emerging, but the process wasn't complete. I needed to take a hard, clear look, and drop all my pretenses. It was all too easy to ignore and cover up what I didn't want to look at or deal with, and, at the same time, look outside for acknowledgement and validation.

And the Universe sent Francis.

My first impression of him was favorable, but not memorable. Maybe that was because his background couldn't have been more different than mine. He came from the tough north side of Philadelphia, a world that was totally unknown to me. He had owned a nightclub and had earned his living as a bartender, before dropping out to search his own spiritual path.

Francis was an astrologer and counselor. Astrology was something I had never put much stock in, but it was a difficult time and I needed help. My husband and I had been separated about six months.

I made an appointment for a reading. When the time came for the session, he greeted me warmly. As we sat down, I felt his bright, hazel eyes penetrate into me, as if he were searing all the way through me to the tip of my toes.

"As a little girl, sometimes you had difficulty understanding your mother," he began.

It wasn't a question, but a statement! I was caught

off guard. How could he know something as personal as that! "You were not an easy child. You challenged her. But on the other hand, she imparted her strength of character to you. Do you appreciate it?" he asked.

"Appreciate it," I thought. "I never thought of it like that."

"She's the perfect teacher for you. That's why you chose her. See here," he said, holding up what was obviously my horoscope. You're very feminine, ultra feminine in the extreme, always yielding, always adapting to your environment—a perfect mirror reflecting back what you think others want from you—especially the men in your life. You can't do that with your mother. She forces you to take a stand, and that's helped you to develop your strength."

His comments rang as clear as a crystal note. I knew what he meant immediately, but I had never thought of it in such a positive way.

"As a child, you were very intuitive. You had many visionary experiences. There were times you knew things before they happened, didn't you?"

I had never told anyone about my childhood experiences. It had always been my secret. A door to my inner self suddenly stood wide open. He had the key. The room was dark and filled with secret parts. I didn't know if I wanted to turn on the light to show everything inside, but I knew at least I didn't want to shut the door.

"Your chart shows that now is a transitional time for you," he said. "It's as if there are two different people— an old self that you are leaving behind, and something new connected to teaching and traveling that will take you to many different parts of the world. That's your destiny," he said, jarring me with his directness. And then, with what sounded like a tone of warning in his voice, he continued. "But you have to become stronger within yourself. Otherwise you will always be absorbed by whomever you are with and lose your identity."

As he spoke, something seemed to explode inside me. His face began to change, and he became enveloped in a luminous glow. In rapid succession, a multitude of images flashed and faded across his face. Sub-personalities, former incarnations, I didn't know which!

I had never had an experience like this before. His words seemed to release an energy within me. Part of me leapt out and connected with him. It was an incredible feeling. Suddenly, with a flash, I was looking inside his body, as if his flesh had dissolved, exposing his bones, organs, and arteries. At the same time, I could feel his intense connection with me. It was magnetic and powerful, and more than I could handle.

I realized with such an intense bond established so suddenly, we must have known each other in other lifetimes. Our connection felt too deep and strong for it to have been a first encounter. It was an uncanny feeling. I felt as if I were standing in front of him being disrobed. He could see right into me. He knew things I never shared with anybody, and hardly admitted to myself. I was fascinated and frightened. I felt an instinctive urge to keep my hand over the light switch to conceal, to hide, to keep things in the shadows I wasn't ready to reveal or felt comfortable about sharing. I had years of being conditioned to be vague and secretive.

It was as if a part of me was shouting, "This is it, This is what you need. Be strong and listen." And at the same time, another part was putting up a defense resenting the invasion of privacy and frightened by stark reality. I found myself reaching the limits of being open and then stepping beyond, still uncomfortable about not being as open and honest as I could.

This is ridiculous, I thought, after the session ended. Why am I hiding things from him. And the more I thought about it, the more uncomfortable I became with myself. Why did I feel it necessary to be covert and couch things in terms that I thought would be acceptable to him?

The next day we met again and took a long walk on the beach. He continued to ask questions. If one answer didn't feel right, he'd ask another question, going deeper. No surface response would do. At some level I knew I needed a crash course in opening myself up, and what I attracted was the most challenging relationship of my life. There was a part of me that wanted to break through my self-imposed ego barriers. I drew a man into my life who would insist on openness, confront me at my point of greatest vulnerability, and challenge my values. Our relationship developed quickly. It was intense, passionate, and characterized by absolute honesty.

There was no way to kid Francis, to tell a half truth or to try to make something better than it was. There was no need to fluff pillows and make everything nice. He challenged me to drop the masks, to drop the guises, to drop the need to have the "right answers." Just tell the truth. I worked on being open, continually uncovering new barriers and dropping my resistance, experiencing new dimensions of freedom. It was challenging, liberating, and scary. No sooner did I feel I had crossed one threshold when there would be another staring me in the face. I continually found myself reaching the limits of my openness, and then allowing myself to move through those awkward moments. And when I found that too threatening or more than I could handle, I simply shut down.

And there were moments of being able to gently let down the ego barriers to reach a new peak in intimacy, openness, and sharing that was totally new for me. It was a level of loving that I had never experienced before. It established a reference point for what it is like not to hide anything, and to be totally accepted. Often though, it took sexuality to reach those depths of intimacy. I could lose myself in Francis for days at a time: we could live in a fantasy world. The value was that we could both talk freely about anything and everything. After years of so many suppressed feelings, it was a welcome relief not to have to pretend, to just be natural, and to love and laugh and be.

But there was a trap. The bed could serve as only a temporary oasis, an escape from the world. It was no lasting solution. The truth was, we were not using our energy productively, but were caught in a treadmill. It wasn't going anywhere. In time, we reached a stalemate.

Nevertheless, Francis was an invaluable guide as I went through the confusion of sorting out my past from the present. We spent hours talking about anything and everything. I was so full of uncertainty about so many things. I relied upon him, instead of trusting my own self.

During this time, Peter and Jason were still important to me. Peter encouraged me to teach, and we often traveled and taught together. It was fascinating, fulfilling, stimulating. When I was with him, I was totally absorbed in Peter and his work. When Jason and I were together, I became caught up in our magical togetherness, and Francis would be out of my mind, out of my thoughts— until I was with him again.

I needed Francis, and he was ready for a committed relationship. But I wasn't. I still enjoyed Peter and Jason, too. Or so I believed. When Francis confronted me with my vacillation, I became soft and yielding, absorbed in him. I was willing to reflect back everything I felt or thought he wanted to see or hear. And it infuriated him.

"How can you love me, and still want to be with other men? You're like a leaf in the wind," he barked. "You don't know where you stand!

It was impossible to be the Pleasing Passive anymore. I didn't want to acknowledge my inconsistencies, so I became the Icy Maiden—cold, aloof, distant, withdrawn. And the colder I became, the more fury it brought out in him. He would explode in volcanic, fiery outbursts that were threatening and confrontational. And while he acted out his rage and resentment, mine stayed inside, because I didn't know how to express my strong feelings. He was my mirror, dramatizing everything inside me I couldn't express. It was high drama—wild extremes and blind projections; fire and ice, not love.

Ultimately we reached an impasse. I didn't want to give him up, and I wanted everything else too! And he insisted that I make a choice. I chose to avoid the issue, and he wanted to force it. We kept pushing at each other. I would dread seeing him, and then surrender to his magnetism and passion. After our love-making, there were still the unresolved questions.

Now, more and more, our attempts to get clear and honest led to confrontations and accusations. We were tearing each other apart, stuck at our crisis point in the relationship and not able to push through it—and still calling it love.

And then I pushed him too far. Things were very heated and tense between us when an opportunity came to do a speaking tour with Peter. It was a welcome relief—and an escape.

For two weeks, I could put Francis behind me, but on the night I returned, the inevitable showdown took place.

I hadn't been back for more than thirty minutes and was still unpacking when Francis called me on the phone. We got into an argument. Irritated, I hung up. Next, I heard a loud, insistent knocking on my door. From the window, I could see Francis, and he was angry! I simply didn't want to deal with it, so I ignored the knocking. The knocking became louder.

"Go away," I called through the door. "We'll talk about it tomorrow."

"This can't wait!" he insisted.

Why didn't he just go away! I didn't want to deal with all this drama and emotion.

Francis went around to the back door to see if it had somehow been left open. Finding it locked, he came back around to the front once again and pounded persistently on the door. Again, I ignored the noise.

"Francis, we'll talk about it tomorrow." The resentment in my voice was obvious.

"The hell we will," he bellowed back. Suddenly, like a scene from a low-budget film and with a loud crash, Francis kicked through the locked door, tearing the jambs from the wall.

"This is crazy," I thought as he strode over the fallen door. "Who does he think he is!" Suddenly I was overwhelmed by how crass this whole situation was. How did I get into this mess anyway!

"Get out of here!" I shouted as I lunged at him and tried to push him back through the ruptured door. "Get out, I never want to see you again!"

Then, both his hands were on me, gripping me hard. Francis yanked me by the nape of the neck and pulled me into the bedroom, and threw me down on the bed. I was too startled to react. He glared down at me, his eyes flashing with anger, his lips trembling with suppressed force. And then, without saying a single word, he turned on his heel and stormed out the door.

I felt violated, angry, bitter—and relieved.

I didn't hear from him for three years. And for a long time, I felt very right about being wronged. How convenient it is to externalize blame. That way we prolong and avoid personal responsibility.

That episode was symbolic. It externalized what was going on inside me. For years I had been conditioned to be vague and secretive; now the door was open. Francis was intent on crashing through all my barriers, and I was equally intent trying to keep them up. I needed my defenses, my safety net, a place to hide. I wanted to hold on to my self-image. I liked being admired, sought after, and considered spiritual. I wanted to be on my mountain top, seeing dreams and visions, not down in the lowlands, dealing with my emotions and facing my fears. It was too painful to look at myself without masks. The door, crashing open, the chain yanked from the wall and splinters flying, was the shock I needed to wake up and take a hard look at the hidden, murky, shadowy parts of myself.

The Healing Process: The Road To Love

For the next three years I worked on strengthening myself. All my primary relationships with men had come to an abrupt end. My father was dead, I was estranged from my brother James, Jason was married, Francis was gone, and my work with Peter was on-again and off-again.

Now, instead of filling up my time with relationships, I spent time with myself, looking within.

I explored the repeating patterns and the "ugly woman" inside me and got to know all her names: the Icy Maiden, the Queen Bee, the Pleasing Passive, Rescue Me, and many others. By embracing these parts, their power over me was diffused. I had touched my depths; I was ready to soar. I spent time loving and supporting myself and noticing when I would step back into dysfunctional modes and relationships that had upheaval, insecurity, hype, the adrenalin rush, uncertainty, and the emotional co-dependency that had been my biggest challenge. Instead, I was transforming my need for life to be stimulating and exciting out of the relationship arena and into the creative edge where it belonged. There is healthy and unhealthy excitement. Even little tendencies within myself, like waiting until the last minute to pack before trips, I was starting to curb. I was noticing what I was doing, forgiving, and accepting that it was okay that I was doing it, and moving into positive changes. Peace, order, and harmony were becoming the order of the day. I was gently moving into a space where I could give and receive more of the Agape love where kindness, caring, and acceptance rule.

It was an important period. And just as I was growing on the inside, in the outer world, my work was expanding. The leaf that had been blowing around in so many directions, subject to the variable currents, had discovered that inside there was a seed. That seed had taken root in the earth. There were still leaves blowing in the wind, but these leaves were on branches connected to a trunk, connected to roots. I had taken ownership of my own inner authority.

During this time, a friend and I decided to do a marathon together. This is a process in which two partners get together for forty-eight hours of uninterrupted time. For the first twenty-four hours, one partner talks, and the other listens. And then for the next twenty-four hours, the roles are reversed. The purpose of the marathon is to create an opportunity to share anything and everything that is on your mind, while your partner agrees to listen, not with the ears, but with the heart, offering no commentary, judgment, or criticism of what is shared. And through the gentle and supportive interaction, profound insight and acceptance of self occurs.

And so in the presence of a trusted friend, I found

myself sharing all my fears, sorrow, fantasies, joys, and confusion about my life, particularly the transitional period. We laughed and we cried. The bonds of trust between us deepened. Insights had space and time to emerge gently, without force. Memories floated up spontaneously from hidden spaces. Patterns and cycles began weaving together. For the first time, I saw clearly the repeated themes playing out in my life.

At one point, I found myself talking about Francis. As I talked about him, I discovered that my feelings of rage, resentment, and self-righteousness had dissolved. I saw him now in a totally different light. I remember what he had said on that very first day. My challenge was to get strong. If I didn't, I would always be absorbed by whoever or whatever was around me.

"You want to do spiritual work?" he said. "The most important work you can do is know yourself. Do that and everything else will fall in place."

I knew now exactly why I had attracted him into my life. He was the perfect complement—someone who insisted on honesty, someone with an obsession for clarity, someone who hated pretense and sham. It was what I needed in my life, in my self.

His own explosive anger, his volcanic outbursts simply mirrored what was bottled up and hidden inside me. All during that time, he was trying to get more connected with his femininity to balance and soften his negative male energy. And so, he attracted me, some-one ultra feminine. On the other hand, I needed to bring out more of my masculinity, more of the authoritarian male energy, to stand up and express my thoughts, feel-ings, and beliefs with confidence. Francis had come into my life to force me to deal with my emotions, and to strengthen what was underdeveloped and weak inside me. He did his job well. We were at opposite ends of the same issue. It was a perfect match.

I completed the marathon, knowing it was a big turning point for me. I was ready to end blame. A few days later I dreamed about Francis, which confirmed my inner change.

In the dream, I walked into a big house. Francis was there. We hugged one another, and as we embraced, I felt warmth and acceptance.

Almost from the beginning moment of seeing Francis, I sensed a genuine change. It can be challenging to shift a relationship which has a history. I was sure we had.

As if to challenge this new level of friendship, we were presented with a test. I had been a little on edge for a few days. I happened to run into Francis and he suggested we take a walk on the beach. On the way we started getting into a disagreement. As the tension mounted, I started to distance myself from Francis, shifting into an old pattern, shutting down and withdrawing. At the same time, I was aware that Francis was trying very hard not to be affected by my mood.

In the past my ice would bring out his fire. All the time I had been withdrawing into my shell, Francis didn't react. There wasn't any anger. There wasn't indifference either. He was genuinely communicating in a supportive way. My mind observed that, but I was too emotionally distant for it to matter.

We got out of the car and walked along the beach silently until we found a spot where we could sit down. It was fall, and the normally crowded beaches were deserted. The only sounds were the rhythmical crashing of the waves and the screech of hungry gulls.

We sat for awhile, looking toward the sea, each absorbed in our own thoughts, our own silence. My anger had become a cold numbness. I was dissatisfied with myself and my inability to feel warm or connected.

Where had all the good feelings gone? How does it end?

Gradually I became aware of Francis. He was smiling, and his face was radiant. Our eyes met and it was as if I could feel his heart saying—"I know you're putting out this coldness. . .and there is nothing more to explain, no more insights, no more words, nothing left that I can give. . .and I Love You."

At that moment, my coldest, most withdrawn, angry self felt that love. And something shifted inside me. In this void of extreme isolation, the pain and separation dissolved in an instant, and I experienced a self-acceptance that I had never felt before. Francis could see through the Icy Maiden to the Real Self. Simultaneously, I realized I didn't need her anymore. I could use her if I wanted to, but I didn't have to be afraid of her coming out.

Suddenly, spontaneously, my heart opened, and the love in me began speaking to the love in him. It was a timeless place where everything becomes known, becomes understood—and everything is love. There was nothing I didn't know at that moment. All that I had struggled with was gone. Everything was clear, as if my mind blended with a higher mind, and that consciousness was speaking for me, speaking through me, pouring forth insights about my life and relationships.

Then I could feel the same energy welling up in Francis. I saw an enormous golden light around him. It filled him, and then I felt a transcendent light enveloping me. I felt a sense of joy and oneness. It was a sacred moment.

He started crying. He had moved through a door, into an experience of love he had never known before. He had taken the first step, and that allowed me to step into it fully, too. I started crying. We were love expressing itself. I had come home to my true self.

Positive Qualities	Challenging Qualities	Response
Openness	Anger	Icy maiden
Integrity	Not rooted	Shrieking
Wisdom	Extremes	war goddess
Understanding	Weak self-image	Seductive
Trust	Critical	siren

Co-Dependency	Gold
Emotional (intensity)	*Take my own power
Mental (decisions)	*Think for self
Spiritual (self-knowledge)	*Openness
	*Develop my own philosophy
	*Self-understanding

Exercises

The Forty-Eight-Hour Marathon

The forty-eight-hour marathon is an opportunity to talk openly about yourself and your life to a supportive partner and to be heard by that person without judgment.

1. For forty-eight hours, you and a partner stay together in a room, going out only for restroom breaks. This time period should be uninterrupted.

2. Arrange for food and drinks to be prepared and brought to you in your room if possible, or make meal preparation simple so that your focus is not taken away from your process.

3. Each partner has twenty-four hours to share his/her life experience. You may literally take the first twenty-four hours (with short stops for sleeping or naps as you need them) or divide the time into six or eight hour intervals and then change partners.

4. When you begin, start with your earliest memories. As you go through your life, if incidents and memories start occurring out of sequence, feel free to

insert them as they arise. Share your experiences, the people in your life, hopes, dreams, fears, challenges, fantasies, pain, joy—whatever has been in your history.

5. When you listen to your partner tell his/her story, be supportive. Avoid the tendency to give opinions or tell how it reminds you or relates to something in your life. Remember, it is to be uninterrupted .

Parent Picture Review

Review your Parent Picture and reassess whether your significant other relationship is the same, similar to or the opposite to your parents' pattern.

Your Own Charts

Consider three important partners in your life, whether they be a boss, a friend, committed partner, lover, etc. After meditating on them for a few minutes, fill in the following charts.

Positive Qualities	Challenging Qualities	Response

Co-Dependency	Gold

Positive Qualities	Challenging Qualities	Response

Co-Dependency	Gold

Positive Qualities	Challenging Qualities	Response

Co-Dependency	Gold

Once a woman claims ownership
of her own inner authority,
she makes a quantum leap into grace,
the highest octave of the feminine.
Her subtler senses awaken: intuition,
insight, and sensitivity to
her own rhythm. Then her laughter
and her aliveness well up from deep
within for she has given birth
to her natural child—Joy.

CHAPTER 10

The Highest Octave of the Feminine

Do You Know Where Bliss Is?

One of the goals of Hindu spirituality is the attainment of Bliss, or nirvana. And so it seemed rather significant that on a recent pilgrimage to India with a small group of women, I found myself in a literal search for Bliss—a small compound in the vast complex of Auroville, a spiritual community in the south of India. We were traveling through India not so much to see what we could see, but to take an inner journey while participating in an outer event, and Auroville was one of the points of interest.

The community, which was inspired by Sri Aurobindo and the Mother, belongs to no one in particular, but to humanity as a whole. In a sense it is an experiment in global integration, representing contributions from more than 120 countries and possessing a population of over 700 residents. The community stretches over acres of lush, green land, the result of

269

careful reforesting and single-handed planting of every tree on the property. It is composed of many compounds or districts, each with a distinctive name, such as Bliss, Silence, and Transformation.

One of the women in our group knew the administrative head of the community. We wanted to visit her, and it seemed a simple enough task. All we had to do was find Bliss, where she happened to live.

Our map showed Bliss, clearly indicated. But, as we approached the entrance to Auroville, we decided to check our direction with several natives who were standing nearby. And they were quick to oblige.

"Can you tell us the way to Bliss?" we asked.

"Sure, sure," they responded, their heads bobbing from side to side. I had yet to learn that Indian head-bobbing and agreeableness has nothing to do with whether or not they know the way. It simply means, "Sure, I will give you directions." It doesn't seem to matter whether the directions are right or wrong.

These directions seemed clear. Down the road two miles, left at the fork in the road, cross the bridge, take the third turn on the left, and the first house on the right will be Bliss!

And all went well. Except when we crossed the bridge, turned left at the third turn off, the first house on the right wasn't Bliss. In fact, there weren't any houses in sight. At the moment of this perplexing revelation, a young man came buzzing down the road in the opposite direction on a motor scooter. We hailed him down, and asked, "Can you tell us how to get to Bliss?"

He stroked his beard thoughtfully. "Ah, Bliss. Yes. Yes. I have heard of it, but I've never been there." And then he smiled, and his head began bobbing, as he said, "But I can tell you—you're going in the wrong direction. It's not west. You must go east." And then he proceeded to give us very explicit directions.

270

We turned the car around and headed back the way we had come. For two bumpy miles we followed the road east, turned left at the fork, crossed the bridge, and at the third turn off, proceeded left. Except when we made the final turn, instead of finding Bliss, we were greeted by an empty field—more exasperation!

Almost as if on cue, a member of the community appeared on the road and headed our way. Again the same question: "Do you know how to get to Bliss?"

"Ah, Bliss," she said, as if remembering it fondly. "I have heard of Bliss but I have never been there. I do know where it is though." The drama being played out was beginning to take on surrealistic overtones.

"But you have come the wrong way. The map is incorrect. You don't go either east or west. Instead you must go north." We got an entirely new set of directions: "Go half a mile down this road and turn right. Go about three miles and then you will come to a clearing. Pass the clearing and there will be a small bridge. Cross over the bridge and the first house on the right is Bliss."

Finally, we thought, she seems to really know the way. Off we went again, following precisely the directions given. And sure enough, just as we crossed over the bridge, we did see the first house on the right. It was a charming cottage with a beautiful, well-tended garden. Delighted, we approached the house and walked under an arbor, as though being welcomed, somehow. It had started to get dark and as we came closer, we could see the light in the kitchen window. Inside there was a young woman with a serene face happily preparing dinner. Perfect, it seemed, for the inhabitant of a domicile called Bliss. We knocked at the door and the woman appeared, warm and gracious.

"Hello. Is this Bliss?" we asked.

"Oh no," she said as she stepped from the door, "This is Serenity."

She wiped her hands on her apron and smiled warmly, "I have never been to Bliss, but I can tell you how to find it."

And for the fourth time, we listened to a new set of instructions. And for the fourth time, we were told to go in a direction opposite to the one we had taken, this time south.

We piled back into the car, and bounced along the rutted road for a short distance, when suddenly one of the women started shouting dramatically, "Stop! Stop the car!"

Diana waved her arms wildly and pointed toward the left to a dirt road much too narrow for our car. "Bliss is down there. I know it is! I know it is!"

"No, Diana, that's not where the woman said. It can't be down there!"

"No, I'm sure it's down that road," she insisted.

"We must go farther," we pleaded.

Not at all deflated by our disbelief, she opened the door and, leaping and dashing like a gazelle, she bounded down the narrow road with great gusto, while we, a chorus of weary women, kept calling her back. She ran for at least a half mile until she saw we weren't about to follow her. Reluctantly, she returned to the car, still insisting she had found the road to Bliss.

It was getting dark, and we all agreed, including Diana, that the only sensible thing to do was to head back to the hospitality center and eat dinner. Hunger and weariness finally overcame our hope and determination. We were ready to give up on ever finding Bliss.

Once at the center, we were directed through the main building to the courtyard. After such a frustrating afternoon, the scene before us was a welcome relief.

Seated by candlelight underneath a beautiful banyan tree were a group of people enjoying some excellent cuisine and lively conversation. The tree was enormous, about fifteen feet in diameter, with majestic branches that reached up to the sky and cascaded down into the earth, rooting again and forming more trunks.

There was something primeval about the tree, something magical and other-worldly about the setting.

Could this be Bliss? The scene had many of the qualities we associate with that word: peace, fellowship, laughter, intimacy, connectedness.

Myriad thoughts ran through my mind. Maybe Bliss didn't really exist except in the imagination. Or maybe it didn't matter whether it existed or not. Maybe the journey was all that mattered. And maybe we wouldn't have recognized it if we had seen it. And maybe the little old weaver that we had seen patiently sitting at his loom the day before, where he sits hour upon hour, still and serene, was Bliss personified. He had never sought it. He had done simple tasks, and he had become it.

Still curious, we asked one of the staff members if indeed there was a Bliss. Sure enough, Diana had been right after all. Hers was the true voice of intuition, but we had listened to so many other voices that we didn't recognize the still, small voice when it came. It had been the perfect parody.

Ownership of Inner Authority

In the beginning of the spiritual journey of almost every woman, there is the need to rely on others for guidance and direction. The others may include parents, mentors, teachers, authority figures, gurus, bosses, therapists, channels, psychics, friends, husbands, mates, pastors, *etc.* That need to depend on others lasts for varying amounts of time. And the degree of the need may range from occasional guidance to total dependency. The irony is that if all the answers come from the outside, there is always the lingering question: Was the answer valid? Was the guidance correct?

As one proceeds along the path, there are stages in one's growth, very much the ones presented in this book, though not necessarily the same ones and not necessarily in the same order, but the challenges are there to face, nevertheless. In time, one turns more within for the answers and looks less to outside sources. And yet, there is a paradox. For one not to seek help from an outside source when it is needed is foolish, and for one not to accept wisdom, in whatever form it comes, is arrogance.

Usually, the growth pattern for a woman is similar to a spiral, with a series of small steps moving upward. At some point, though, in almost every woman's life, she is faced with a moment that can be a quantum leap in consciousness. A quantum leap differs from the spiral in that the spiral has the same diameter all the way up. With the quantum leap, however, the whole consciousness expands. We catapult into a subtler vibration. Our view of everything changes. We feel connected with the spirit and the fullness of our own being.

We have been lifted to the highest octave of the feminine: Though this shift in consciousness can be precipitated in a variety of ways, often the catalyst for the shift is an experience that challenges us to take full command of our inner authority. It can be a single moment or a specific time period when we are required to gather at the center of our heart all we most truly know and with it rise up and say yes to life and yes to the task set before us. It is the major initiation into womanhood.

One of the classic stories about a woman facing the unknown and having the courage of her own inner convictions is told in the myth of Psyche. Psyche is given four tasks to perform in order to redeem herself. (Gathering the fleece from the rams and sorting out seeds have already been mentioned in earlier chapters). The fourth challenge is the most difficult. She is required to descend into Hades, the subconscious realm, and face a series of challenges. We cannot soar higher than we are willing to descend. She is not given this task, though, until she has gathered the necessary strength from the preceding challenges. Among other things, she is instructed to get the flask of beauty ointment from Persephone and bring it back to Aphrodite. She is also told not to open the flask.

Aprodite, the oldest of the goddesses, holds a position of authority on Mt. Olympus that was not to be denied. She was powerful and she was influential. Certainly, Psyche knew that to violate in any way her instructions would have severe consequences. She would lose all that she had worked so hard to regain. Not only that, but she had already passed through strenuous tasks and had almost finished her long process of redeeming herself. Everything was at stake. It would be foolish to jeopardize herself at this point.

But Psyche, responding to her own inner promptings, decides to open the flask anyway. She immediately falls into a deep, dream-like sleep. It would seem that at this moment, alas, all would be lost. Instead Eros, who from the beginning has represented her anima, swoops down and unexpectedly lifts her to Mt. Olympus where she is welcomed no longer as just a mortal but as a goddess in her own right. She has emerged out of her illusion and limitation, her narcissism and superficiality, and has grown into full-bloom womanhood. She marries Eros, symbolic of the integration of her female-male parts and from that union, a child is born, appropriately called joy.

The last step in Psyche's journey is replete with

symbolism. There is no need to comment on all that could be said, but only to focus on what is relevant in understanding that moment when a woman is her most genuine self.

Is This The Big One?

The myth presents some important insights of the archetypal dimensions in a woman's journey. As women, we face more than one turning point in our lives. But the moment of initiation into womanhood is accompanied by a cluster of components that set that experience apart from all others. If any of these components are missing, the experience may be close to or similar to a big initiation—it may be an important step, significant and strengthening—but it is not that major moment.

The most important component in the initiation into womanhood is that moment when you recognize that there is no authority but your own inner authority, and you act on it. It is indeed a holy moment, and you stand alone. Characteristically, no one is there to support you, either immediately before the experience, during the experience, and often for some time afterwards. There is purpose, even in that. You must stand for something, by something, in something for once in your life. And you must do it alone. It is as though the angels themselves are held back in waiting. They wait for you to be who are you are. Psyche experienced it like a sleepless death. It is a death, a death to the old self, a death to naivete and self-absorption, a death to immaturity. The commitment is to your own inner being— to life itself and the tasks life puts before you.

The moment itself may not be as difficult as others have been earlier in our lives. In fact, it may not even be experienced as a quantum leap, except in retrospect and by comparison. But we have been developing our spiritual muscles little by little, even though we are seldom aware of the progress we have been making. When the time comes for the big leap, we are, at that moment, so vertical, so connected, so aligned, that the decision is spontaneous and natural. There is seldom room for ambivalence or doubt.

The response is never reactionary. It is never against, done to retaliate or hurt or undermine or defy, or done from some other equally negative motive. It is, always, a movement toward something—toward truth. It uplifts, just by its very nature.

The second major component of the initiation is that both the timing and the decision must align. There is no correct response, and there is the right response. What makes it right is that it is true for you. Because the response comes from a deep place within, it may defy rational mind. It may seem like heresy or be labeled immature, irrational, inappropriate, irresponsible, too responsible, too committed, too emotional, not emotional enough, *etc.* Reactions may be mixed, and it won't matter. The intent was never to please others. What will matter is that it is right for you.

The decisions, themselves, can even be contradictory. It may be adopting a handicapped child; marrying a man ten years your junior; staying in a relationship that everyone advises you to leave; committing to spiritual growth; leaving a secure job for a much lower paid one that is more fulfilling; finally standing up to your mother-in-law and defining boundaries; going back to graduate school at forty; deciding at thirty never to have children; deciding at forty to have a baby; educating your children with or without help from anyone else.

Not only must the answer be right for you, but there must be the right timing for that response. Timing means sensing the right moment, being neither pre-mature nor too hesitant. If either timing or decisions are off, that would indicate that we are not yet sensitive to our own rhythm. Then more experience is required, and life will present another opportunity later on that will be the right moment.

The Highest Octave Of The Feminine

Once we have passed the initiation of responding to our own inner authority, it doesn't mean life becomes clear, wonderful, and easy. Rather, it means that our souls, our psyches begin to resonate to a higher octave of the feminine. We have crossed the threshold and we enter another vortex of energy—one that gives us more access to wisdom, grace, and joy. We stand at the center of our own universe living our dream, and from that van-tage point, all people and experiences become accurate communicators for exactly what we need to learn.

The outer is clearly reflecting the inner. Life is our teacher, and brings to us everything we need to learn. The true lessons are mastered when we realize all the answers lie within. At this moment, confirmations and adjustments are realized much quicker than before. Synchronicity, which may have happened only occa-sionally, now occurs much more often and with greater meaning, because we are sensitive enough now to be open and to embrace those experiences, listening for the lessons life teaches. We trust our intuition to know how to respond. Most importantly, our heart has been opened. It includes more, more of ourself and more of others, more of life. There is so much more to express, to feel, and to be. When we begin to experience this grace in our lives, the only response is to bow head silently and be thankful.

Grace is the highest octave of the feminine, and the

greatest protection. Grace helps us see more clearly, and offers options. It is an avenue to change easily and quickly rather than painfully and slowly. It is as though life is laid out for us in a perfect path, we need only be thankful for every moment and follow the path our own wisdom points us toward. We no longer need to depend on anything outside ourself as a source of well-being. Our laughter and our aliveness well up from deep within, for we have given birth to our child—Joy.

Little clues occur to reinforce our awareness that we are on the right track. Recently when I came back from the tour to India, on the spur of the moment, I called a friend of mine, an author in California. At that moment, he was writing about India. Two weeks later, I called him again on the spur of the moment. This time he had just written a sentence about Virginia Beach!

What do these things prove or mean? They reinforce our confidence that our inner self is attuned to something larger and more orderly, than our conscious mind knows.

Sometimes, a series of events will carry one theme. For example, I was recently given a beautiful hand-crafted angel and promptly found a special place for it in my home. Two days later a note came in the mail from someone with the words, "Thank you for being an angel in my life." I was touched. And two days later again a friend in Holland wrote, "This is your year and an angel points the way." And in another few days, a gift arrived in the mail: It was a book on angels!

One thing that is learned quickly: God has a sense of humor. Recently, I was leaving Gatwick Airport in London en route back to the States. I had purposely waited to be among the last of the boarding passengers, promptly presented my boarding card, and suddenly froze when I realized that I didn't have my pocketbook. The plane was only fifteen minutes away from take-off and retrieving my lost bag was not the top priority for the airplane agents. My mind raced quickly to where I had been; airline check-in desk, foreign exchange desk, security check...ah, yes, security check. It might be there. I dashed back to the gate with great anxiety since all the money which I had earned during the last month, plus credit cards, were in the bag. Waiting there for me was a smiling, uniformed, airplane official. "Miss Marlow," he said, "did you lose something?" How did he know my name? "Well," he continued, "It would take someone with a name like that to drop your pocketbook, money and all, and to have someone with a name like mine to pick it up." I wondered what my name had to do with it. My eyes suddenly noticed the name tag on his uniform—Marlowe. We both chuckled. "I always wondered when I would meet my long-lost rich relative." He was referring to the wad of bills I had rolled up, right-brain fashion, inside the bag. I assured him that unfortunately all of the bills weren't large ones.

Those precious moments are saying "you are on track." And when we aren't, we are told that too! A friend reported that she backed out of her driveway as she had done hundreds of times, except that she didn't see the car parked behind her and went smack into it. It was a reminder that she was so focused on her thoughts and what she was doing that she was missing a lot of life around her. That day she noticed the sunset for the first time in many days.

The Ladybug

One of the most beautiful examples of synchronicity occurred during a retreat experience I led at Virginia Beach. It happened with a man—proof that males can experience the higher octave of the feminine also.

The last afternoon of the retreat was spent in silence, and each person could go wherever he or she chose: on the beach, to the woods, in the room, *etc*. The focus was to be inner, not outer. Everyone was asked to find some object that captured their attention, something that seemed to symbolize where they were in their life or what they were feeling inside. They were not to use a lot of effort to find the object, but just allow that special something to speak to them. The objects were to be both personal and symbolic.

The experience of one particular person was profound. Tom walked along the beach and was drawn to an old, beat-up copper penny lying almost hidden in the sand, well-weathered by sun and salt. He leaned down to pick it up, not knowing exactly why and continued down the beach. As he walked, he noticed a puddle of water in the sand. The ocean water had been captured somehow in this little crevice. In the puddle struggled a tiny ladybug, unable to move up on the sand and mustering all her strength to keep from drowning. A compassionate chord was struck inside Tom. He took out the copper penny, which he had since stuffed in his pocket, and because it was the most precious thing he had, he placed it gently under the little creature, lifted it up carefully and then placed it down on the nearby sand where it had a chance of a new life. At that moment he thought he heard his name being called out, but dismissed it as pure imagination.

When Tom came back to the retreat house several hours later, there was a phone message waiting for him. His grandmother, who had been the most important nurturing figure in his life, had died. At the same time he was on the beach helping the ladybug cross over the water, Tom's grandmother had quit struggling in her pain-racked body and had crossed over to another life. There was not a dry eye in the group.

Going Home To See Where You Are

There are some important milestones in every woman's life: marriage, birth of a child, the first job. Some are filled with joy and excitement; others, by their very nature, carry mixed blessings. Such was an experience last summer. My father had been dead for several years and my mother, though formidable in vitality, was moving on in years. The time had come, she decided, to sell the family home and move into a retirement community.

The feeling of forever leaving the family home was a milestone that I hadn't anticipated. With all my travelings and wanderings, I hadn't been there very much in recent years. But still, it was home and an anchor. Now, for the first time in all my life, it wouldn't be there anymore.

What would that be like? Almost all my growing up years had been spent there. I had only known two homes in my life.

Somehow, I was the one delegated to help sort out the household items and paraphernalia. Sorting out the childhood treasures was a reminder of precious memories: colored wooden blocks carved with letters of the alphabet; Easter baskets, pink bows, and green stuffing still in place, but no longer with a delicious nest of foil-wrapped chocolate eggs; my brother's beloved marbles. What a delight to experience these once again, yet bittersweet all the while.

It was a final farewell to all of it. My feelings were mixed. I was happy about my mother's enthusiasm for her new life, yet I was inwardly reflective at the same time. Sometimes you go home to see where you are. It was that kind of weekend.

To add to the feelings of nostalgia, my family had been invited to a reunion at the little church in Browntown, where my father grew up. Browntown is a tiny community nestled in the foothills of the Blue Ridge Mountains. As a child, the town seemed confined and limiting, and I was only too glad when we didn't have to live there. Now, on this weekend, it seemed tranquil and charming.

The Browntown Church is a white, clapboard structure with plush green lawns—right out of a Currier & Ives painting.

My mother, two brothers, my sister-in-law, and I were greeted warmly and seated in the back pew. As we settled into our seats, I had a tingly sensation that happens in my body whenever there is about to be an important scene played out. It is as though I am being told to particularly take notice, that the next cosmic drama about to unfold has been staged just for me. My intuition proved correct.

A feeling of peacefulness suffused the little church, and my eye was drawn to the shiny countenances of several in the congregation, and then to the radiant face of the visiting minister as he walked to the pulpit.

With sparse white hair and a frail, almost birdlike delicateness, the minister appeared to be seventy years or older. But his eyes sparkled and his voice was clear and well-honed from years of homilies and counseling.

"I came with a sermon and a scripture reading all prepared," he announced, "but just this moment the Spirit told me to change the topic and the text." He opened his bible, and with a well-trained eye and sureness borne of familiarity, he thumbed through the pages until he came to a familiar spot.

The people seemed a little more attentive. A few coughs punctuated the silence. And as he began to read, I was delighted and surprised. The spontaneous guidance of the Spirit had led him to a passage that has always been my favorite: "I have come to give you life that you might have life more abundantly." He formed the words slowly and with devotion, weaving a texture of respect and intimacy into the words of the Master.

When he looked up from the book, his face glowed with contentment and serenity.

"When I was a young boy, I tended sheep for my father. And one day, when I was alone in the hills, an angel appeared to me and told me that my life's work was to be one of service, of sharing Christ's message. Because it was one of the purest moments of my life, I have always tried to follow it."

A surge of energy shot through me. It sounded so familiar. It was like my story. This clear knowing, from the very beginning, of what my life's work was to be. How does it come so young?

After the service we shared one of those incredible country meals which city people can only dream about. Table after table was laden with homemade fare, everything delicious and bountiful. When we left, I felt nourished on all levels. Simple people, simple words, simple truth—yet profound.

The ride back to Front Royal was on a windy country road. That day it seemed particularly peaceful and gentle, a perfect reflection of the way I was feeling on the inside. There was such a beautiful synchronicity in the letting go of the family home and the reconnecting at the same time with my roots. The outer symbol could go now, because the inner connection was much stronger. It was from these people, this land, this heritage, that I had my beginnings. And it was here, as well, that there had been that early and powerful connection to Spirit.

I could feel my heart expanding to embrace and hold so much more, not only these early beginnings but all the experiences in my life. How similar we as women are, no matter what our roots, our origins, our experiences. Somewhere along our path, we begin to own and embrace all our parts, those parts we consider beautiful equally with those parts we consider not so beautiful; the Bitches, the Dragon Fights, the betrayals, the hurts and pains. Whatever has been our greatest struggle is transformed into our greatest strength. All our experiences begin to hold so much more hope, so much more promise.

For a moment, there was a fleeting image of Krishna, the Hindu figure of Christ, dancing on the serpent. I had seen this image several times in India and had never understood what it meant. Of course, it suddenly became clear. Dance on all of it. That is the joy.

By accepting who we are, we emerge out of limitations and open to the highest octave of the feminine. We then dance with an open heart, and we dance with great joy.